ADVENTUROUS PUB WALKS
IN
OXFORDSHIRE

Roger Noyce

COUNTRYSIDE BOOKS
NEWBURY BERKSHIRE

Designed by Peter Davies, Nautilus Design
Maps by the author

Photographs by Margaret Noyce

Cover photograph of the Manger, near Woolstone,
supplied by Julian Comrie

Produced through MRM Associates Ltd., Reading
Typeset by Techniset Typesetters, Newton-le-Willows
Printed by Woolnough Bookbinding Ltd., Irthlingborough

CONTENTS

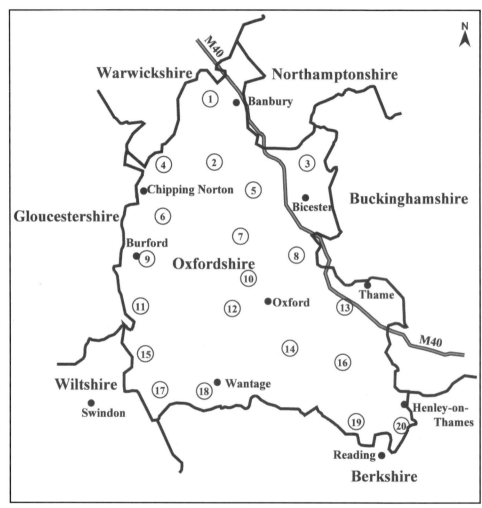

AREA MAP SHOWING THE LOCATION OF THE WALKS

INTRODUCTION

Oxfordshire is a most beautiful county, where you can combine adventurous walking with visits to fascinating places that have connections with a broad spectrum of interesting historical events, one of the most important being the Civil War. There are many castles and large country houses scattered over the county, beautiful villages to meander through and historic English pubs to visit.

Red kites soaring majestically over tree-covered hilltops; colourful narrow-boats making their way along a picturesque canal; attractive villages of honey-coloured stone and streets of thatched cottages; gentle hills inviting you to share their stunning views; and the magical River Thames offering a picture of modem leisure with boats of all shapes and sizes – these are just some of the delights on offer in the historic county of Oxfordshire.

The twenty circular walks in this book are based around good pubs serving appetising, satisfying food, and they are sufficiently long and demanding to present a challenge, although you do not have to be super-fit to tackle them. I cannot offer you the muscle-straining, calf-killing slogs that may be found in some parts of the country, but in this seemingly unchanging rolling landscape there are adventures and enjoyments of a different kind to be had. Oxfordshire is a county of peaceful villages where pretty thatched cottages and beautiful churches may be reached on narrow lanes still relatively free of traffic.

Ranging in length from $6^1/_4$ to $12^1/_2$ miles, the routes can be enjoyed equally by those new to walking and regular walkers. Stroll through the attractive Cotswold villages of Great Tew and North Newington, where thatched cottages line the streets. Walk along public footpaths through the Great Park at Woodstock, where you can enjoy superb views of Blenheim Palace; experience the sight of red kites soaring above Mapledurham as you stroll towards its fine Elizabethan manor house. At Dorchester, the ancient abbey dominates the village and the walk takes you along the banks of the river past more beautiful cottages. The walk along the famous Ridgeway near Woolstone offers the opportunity to see possibly the oldest of Britain's chalk hill figures – the White Horse. The Oxford Canal was built in 1790 to link the River Thames with Midlands industry and on several of the walks you can saunter along its fine towpath.

Adventure with me and visit these fascinating historic places, taking time to stop for refreshments at one of the county's ancient pubs. All of the routes incorporate public rights of way, where there is an onus upon every walker always to follow the Country Code, to look after our precious countryside and to protect the environment for future generations. Most of the walks cross farmland at some point and so the usual countryside courtesies must be observed, such as closing gates behind you. Footpaths in Oxfordshire are generally well waymarked and old wooden stiles are gradually being replaced by metal kissing gates – a situation that is constantly changing, so you may find that improvements have been made since I walked the routes for this book.

The surface on many of the footpaths is generally good so that persons of mature years and families with young children should have little difficulty. The weather in this country is well known to be unpredictable and it is important always to have the right clothing. In hot weather always take a hat with you as protection against the sun is essential, as is a bottle of water. In wet weather, or during the winter months, be prepared for muddy stretches on some footpaths. If it is really cold, several layers of thinner garments are warmer than one thick one; also, they allow you to change according to the temperature during the walk.

I am pleased to invite you to stroll along the lovely footpaths in the beautiful county of Oxfordshire and to visit some of its pubs and inns. I wish you many happy adventures.

Roger Noyce

PUBLISHER'S NOTE

*W*e hope that you obtain considerable enjoyment from this book; great care has been taken in its preparation. Although at the time of publication all routes followed public rights of way or permitted paths, diversion orders can be made and permissions withdrawn.

We cannot, of course, be held responsible for such diversion orders and any inaccuracies in the text which result from these or any other changes to the routes nor any damage which might result from walkers trespassing on private property. We are anxious though that all details covering the walks are kept up to date and would therefore welcome information from readers which would be relevant to future editions.

The simple sketch maps that accompany the walks in this book are based on notes made by the author whilst checking out the routes on the ground. They are designed to show you how to reach the start, to point out the main features of the overall circuit and they contain a progression of numbers that relate to the paragraphs of the text.

However, for the benefit of a proper map, we do recommend that you purchase the relevant Ordnance Survey sheet covering your walk. The Ordnance Survey maps are widely available, especially through booksellers and local newsagents.

THE AMERICAN CONNECTION

Distance:
7³/₄ miles

Starting point:
The village pond in
Wroxton.
GR 414417

Map: OS Explorer 191 – Banbury, Bicester & Chipping Norton

How to get there: Wroxton is about 3¹/₄ miles west of
Banbury. Leave Banbury on the A422 (Stratford-upon-Avon
road). Go left into the village centre, passing the church to
arrive near the North Arms pub and the village pond.

THE VILLAGE POND IN WROXTON

A fine walk in North Oxfordshire starting from the beautiful village of Wroxton, where honey stone, thatched cottages are grouped around the village pond, and signs warn drivers to watch out for ducks crossing the road. From the village, tracks and lanes lead through Padsdon Bottom and over delightful Cotswold countryside for the classic view of Broughton Castle. On to picturesque North Newington where time appears to stand still and the Blinking Owl pub may delay you. An 'eyecatcher' archway and then an obelisk are passed and you will get a good view of Wroxton College – the former home of Lord North (Prime Minister 1770–1782), who has gone down in history as the man who gave away the Americas.

9

The Saye & Sele Arms like much of Broughton, was once part of Broughton Castle estate and it appears that its name has changed over the years, seemingly to reflect the title of the owner of the castle. First licensed as a pub in 1780, it was called the Twistledon Arms between 1812 and 1826. A recognisance of £10 sterling applied in 1812 and had increased to £20 by 1826. The innkeeper who put up the amount was required to keep a respectable house during the year, i.e. no fighting, gambling or loose women! The Twistledon Arms became the Saye & Sele Arms in about 1820, then in 1848 it was back to the Twistledon Arms. Today it is the Saye & Sele Arms once again.

The attractive Cotswold stone pub is very popular and walkers can expect a warm welcome. A wide range of bar snacks and restaurant meals are produced in a brand new kitchen designed to ensure a high standard of food. The real ales Wadworth 6X, Adnams Southwold, plus two guest ales, are on tap.

> **Food is served** *from 12 noon to 2 pm every day and in the evenings on Monday to Saturday from 7 pm to 10 pm; no food is served on Sunday evening. There is a large, safe play area for children.*
> *Telephone: 01295 263348; website: www.sayeandselearms.co.uk;*
> *e-mail: mail@sayeandselearms.co.uk*

 *The Walk*

① From the village pond, proceed up Main Street. passing lovely thatched cottages.

Wroxton offers the quintessential English village scene. Spare time to stroll through the village and see its wonderful cottages, village pond (with ducks) and thatched pub. Behind the walls is Wroxton Abbey (now Wroxton College) set amid beautiful lawns, lakes, gardens and woodland. Henry James (1843-1916), the famous American writer, was a regular visitor to this remarkable 17th-century Jacobean manor house and for him it was part of the essence of England. It is now occupied by the Fairleigh Dickinson University and is not open to the public.

After about 275 yards, go left and up a path to the left of Wroxton C of E primary school building. Proceed over a couple of stiles along the left edge of a field and continue past barns to a farm gate and a track. Do not go through the gate but turn right along a headland track to reach and cross a road.

Follow the fingerpost direction over a couple of cultivated fields to a hedge stile and go left along a clear track/footpath – delightful easy walking along the top of **Padsdon Bottom**, with a stream in the valley to your right. After about 1/2 mile the path descends to lead through a farm gate. Head left onto a wide, fenced grass track and at the field end veer right and then left through a hand-gate – **Tithe Farm** is up to the right. Continue ahead to the left of **Claydonhill Covert** then, after about 150 yards, bear right into the trees, maintaining your direction on a bridle-path inside the covert edge. At the end of the covert, arc right and take the bridle-path through the trees to come into the open and reach the top of **Claydon Hill** for a fine view over the surrounding countryside. Descend by the side of the hedge to a farm track and the road. Go left along the grass verge of the road for almost 200 yards. (1 1/2 miles)

② Cross over the road just before the entrance to **The Knowle** and proceed over a stile into pastureland. Follow the fingerpost direction, walking to the immediate left of the clump of trees on **Welshcroft Hill,** then descending through a farm gate/stile to arrive on the farm lane by **Broughton Grounds Farm**. Head left along the quiet road for just over 1/2 mile – the lane bends left near to some houses at **Castle Brow**. Look out for a fingerpost signed 'North

THE SAYE & SELE ARMS, FIRST LICENSED AS A PUB IN 1780

11

Newington ³/₄' and here turn right through a farm gate onto a clear track by trees. At the barn go left across a large field and proceed through a hand-gate into the grounds of **Broughton Park**. Follow the direction of the waymark, bearing slightly left. As you reach the brow of the hill you will have a magical view of Broughton Castle, which was a location for part of the film *Shakespeare in Love*.

The moated Broughton Castle was erected in 1306 by Sir John de Broughton as a fortified stone manor house. Some 70 years later it passed to William de Wykeham and in 1405 Thomas Wykeham added battlements and a fine gatehouse. The granddaughter of Sir William's sister married Sir William Fiennes, the second Lord Saye and Sele, in 1451. During the Civil War, William Fiennes, the eighth Lord Saye and Sele, opposed Charles I and raised a regiment that fought at Edgehill in 1642. After the battle, the castle was captured. Following a short period on Lundy Island, William returned and it became the Saye and Sele family home. The current Lord and Lady Saye moved into the castle in 1968 and it is now open to the public between May and September each year on Sunday and Wednesday afternoons only. In summer, it offers a picture-postcard scene

with colourful water-lilies filling its lovely moat. The nearby 14th-century St Mary's church contains a painted tomb of Sir John de Broughton.

Enjoy this lovely view and descend the hill, aiming towards **St Mary's church**. Enter the churchyard and proceed to the right of the church on a stone slab path up to the main road in **Broughton**. (1³/₄ miles)

③ Go left along the pavement to find the **Saye & Sele Arms**, but to continue the route proceed ahead along the pavement, passing by some fine old buildings (1899) and a bus stop. Just after passing **Danvers Road**, go left over a stile at a fingerpost signed 'North Newington ³/₄' – North Newington is always three-quarters of a mile away! Pass through the stables area and cross over a footbridge to walk to the left of a well hidden sewage works. Turn right over a stile onto the entrance drive to the works and continue ahead over the field corner to a lane. Turn right along the lane for 300 yards, bear left then go through a farm gate set in the right-hand field hedge into pastureland. Now aim towards a round dovecote sited near **Park Farm**. Bear left near the dovecote and go over a stile onto a green lane that leads into the village of **North Newington**. Go left along **Park Lane** into the main street, passing the **Blinking Owl** pub. Turn right, and head up the first lane on the right. The lane arcs right and you then proceed ahead through a gateway to a children's play area and onto a footpath at the back of the village houses to reach another lane. Cross over the lane and go over the stile opposite, then go down the field to the right of **Sorbrook Barn Cottage**. Exit via a stile at the field's bottom left corner. Continue by going over a couple of bridges across a stream and then follow the left edge of a young plantation of oak and beech trees. (2 miles)

④ At the top of the plantation go left at a junction of paths onto the field headland. This is the **Banbury Fringe Circular Walk** and there are fine views to enjoy. Pass to the left of **Withycombe Farm** and continue along the farm drive, with the town of Banbury to your right. At the third field hedge go left onto a permissive path to reach the intriguing **Drayton Archway**, pausing to enjoy a pleasing view that embraces an obelisk standing proud on the hill ahead.

The Drayton Archway was designed by Sanderson Miller, a leading exponent of Gothic Revival. It is a real 'eyecatcher' and sited so as to be seen from the gardens of the then Wroxton Abbey.

Bear right past the archway and then left onto a farm track descending gently towards a stream – lovely views ahead. Ascend the hill past the obelisk and enjoy the splendid prospect of Wroxton College and its attractive gardens.

The obelisk was erected in 1739 to commemorate the visit of Frederick, Prince of Wales in 1739.

Proceed over the stiles to the left of the gardens and go through the farm gate and then ascend the bank to go through a hand-gate into pastureland and on to the Gothic dovecote.

Built by Sanderson Miller in 1745 the Gothic dovecote stands on the highest ground near to the former abbey. It has loop windows, battlements, a fine banner-type weathervane and was also an 'eyecatcher'.

From the gate bear right along the well used path to a kissing gate and descend by the edge of the college gardens to return to the duck pond in **Wroxton** village. (2¹/₂ miles)

Date walk completed:

SOUTH NEWINGTON
AND GREAT TEW

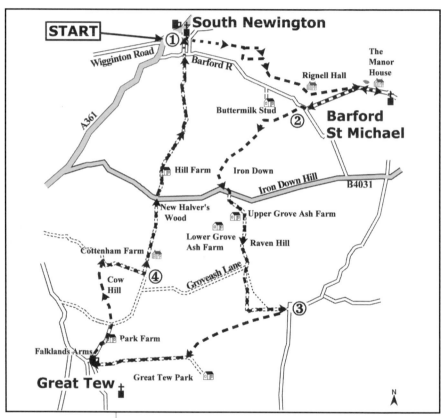

Distance:
9½ miles

Starting point:
The high street in
South Newington.
GR 407333

Map: OS Explorer 191 – Banbury, Bicester & Chipping Norton

How to get there: South Newington is on the A361
road, 6 miles south-west of Banbury. Park with
consideration at the bottom of the high street in the village.

*T*his is a fine hill walk in north Oxfordshire, starting from the peaceful village of South Newington, where honey-coloured stone cottages surround the village green. It is an adventure into the Cotswolds across open land to the neighbouring village of Barford St Michael to see its lovely old manor house surrounded by fishing lakes. There are pleasing views to enjoy as you ascend to the top of Iron Down and on the approach to the picturesque village of Great Tew. As you walk by the side of Great Tew Park you may see lapwings nesting in the fields. Stunning thatched cottages greet your arrival in Great Tew and you walk past a number of them before climbing Cow Hill for a fine view of the village. A super walk with plenty of scenery to enjoy.

The Falkland Arms – an award winning inn – is a regular haunt of local walkers and you are guaranteed a warm welcome. It dates back to the 16th century, when it was originally called the Horse and Groom. Set at the end of a row of thatched properties, it has a front garden that is a delightful place to sit in to enjoy the unique atmosphere of the Cotswolds. In winter, you can sit by the inglenook fireplace and admire a fantastic collection of mugs and jugs that hang from the ceiling and a selection of clay pipes and snuff that are on sale.

During the week, opening hours are from 11.30 am to 2.30 pm (12 noon to 3 pm on Saturday and Sunday) and from 6 pm to 11 pm (7 pm to 10.30 pm on Sunday). Old Timer, 6X and Henley's IPA are the regular ales and there are always guest ales available – seven real ales that vary from week to week. The pub has been awarded a Cask Marque. Inch's Harvest Dry is the cider on tap and there is a large selection of wines and whiskies.

Food is served *between 12 noon and 2 pm and from 7 pm to 8 pm every day of the week. There is a traditional country bar menu, with hand-raised pork pies and beef and ale pie being two of the favourites.*
Children are allowed in the lounge and garden only; dogs are permitted but must be kept under control and on leads at all times.
Walkers who are customers may use the car park.
Telephone: 01608 683653; website: www.falklandarms.org.uk; e-mail address: sjcourage@btconnect.com

WALKING PAST THE GATEWAY TO GREAT TEW PARK

 *The Walk*

① Stroll down to the bottom of the **High Street** in **South Newington** and then turn right.

South Newington is a Saxon settlement. Inside the church of St Peter ad Vincula are some most remarkable wall paintings that are well worth seeing before you start your walk. The Virgin and Child of about 1330 is one of the finest paintings in any English church. The Virgin is crowned and in her left hand she holds a wand or rod surmounted by a fleur-de-lys, now rather faint against the highly decorated background. Her robe and mantle fall in elegant folds. The painting of the murder of Thomas à Becket is badly damaged, though, for Henry VIII objected to Becket as a symbol of church resistance to the crown and ordered that all images of and references to Becket be expunged. It remains, however, one of the most interesting medieval wall paintings in England.

At the end of **Green Lane** bear left and proceed along a walled pathway into open countryside via a stile. Walk the pleasant footpath until you arrive at the third stile and a large cultivated field – the **River Swere** is in the valley to your left and you may see a heron if you are lucky.

Go over the stile. The public footpath leads you into the middle of the field, where a right turn will take you to a field hedge stile. Alternatively you may prefer to go to the right up a wide headland path that circles the edge of the field to reach the same stile. At this stile follow the waymarker direction and cross over a stream via a footbridge then cross the next field to its top left-hand corner, where you ascend through trees to reach a

lane near to **Rignell Farm** and **Hall**. Immediately after passing by the hall, go left over pastureland and a cultivated field to reach the South Newington road on the edge of the village of **Barford St Michael**. (Head left up the road if you want to see the small fishing lakes and the **Manor House** on the edge of the village, then retrace your steps along the minor road up to the main road.) (1½ miles)

② Cross over the road and go over the stile opposite. Follow the fingerpost direction and walk generally south-west, crossing several stiles. As you near **Buttermilk Stud** (on your right) the path hugs the field hedge and then arcs left and

THE AWARD WINNING FALKLAND ARMS

you can enjoy a lovely stretch of walking as you gently ascend the side of a hill, crossing several fields with a pleasing view over **South Newington** to your right. At the top of the ascent you will be on the edge of **Iron Down** and can then walk a clear green path to reach the **B4031** road.

Head left along the grass verge of the road for about 75 yards then cross over and walk down the driveway towards **Lower Grove Ash Farm**. Initially this is a tarmac drive which you leave by bearing left, walking to the left of **Upper Grove Ash Farm** buildings. Walk this clear track (**Groveash Lane**), going towards **Raven Hill**. A farm gate leads into beautiful open countryside and the main part of the lane, where there are a couple of waymarker posts. Proceed ahead, crossing the main track onto a footpath that leads into the trees, then continue ahead onto a hedged track going southwards. At the track junction, go left and walk along the field headland up to a lane. (2³/₄ miles)

③ Do not go over the stile onto the lane but turn round and walk on the clear footpath that runs almost parallel with the original track, now going south-west and aiming for a stile in the hedge. Go over the stile and take the clear, well-walked path, maintaining your generally south-west direction. Cross over the rather dilapidated sleeper bridge and continue over two further fields arcing generally left towards the corner of a Cotswold stone wall. Bear right through the farm gate and take the headland farm track by the stone wall, enjoying the lovely view over Walker's Hill to your right. Lapwings often congregate and nest in this field so please read the RSPB notice on the gate and take care not to interfere with any birds on the field. You will pass by the disused gateway into **Great Tew Park** where superb trees have space to spread their wonderful limbs. After walking the headland for about ³/₄ mile you arrive near the **Falkland Arms** inn in the village of **Great Tew**.

A stroll around the beautiful village of Great Tew is a special treat. It is privately owned and the post office, pub, school and picturesque thatched cottages which border the village green are a true delight. Many of the cottage gardens are edged by neatly trimmed hedges, which were part of the planting scheme of John Claudius Loudon, who was responsible for Colonel Stratton's estate, of which Great Tew was a part. St Michael's and All Angels' church sports an Italianate gateway which is believed to have come from Tew Park.

Head right to go past the inn and

the fine thatched post office. Continue by strolling along **Brook Road**, taking time to admire the many cottages boasting more thatch. The road bends left and descends past **Park Farm**.

At the bottom of the road leave the road/track and proceed ahead over a stile and ascend **Cow Hill** – a fairly steep climb but, if you take a look behind, you will be rewarded with an excellent view over **Great Tew**. Continue ahead over the stile by the farm gate and now descend the other side of **Cow Hill**. After going over a further stile you will arrive at what is shown on the map as a lane (in practice it is little more than a farm track). Turn right onto it and after about 600 yards you will arrive back on the main track. (3¼ miles)

④ Head left along the main track, which soon becomes a tarmac lane, passing by the superb residence of **Cottenham Farm** with its fine lake. The track is rather special in the spring for you pass by **Pool Spinney** (on your left) where wild white anemones and bluebells cover the bank and then on your right more anemones, celandines and bluebells make a superb carpet. As you walk along the track the bluebells in **New Halver's Wood** will catch your eye and then you will be back at the **B4031** road once again.

Cross the road and go up the driveway towards **Hill Farm**. Just before the farm complex bear left through a farm gate and proceed along the bridleway to the left of farm buildings. You will soon be back on the main farm track that stretches along the top of the hill. (Across to your right you will see the path you ascended to Iron Down on your outward route.) Then descend left past some trees into the valley. Follow the waymarker directions that take you initially to the left of the field hedge and then arc right to continue up a hedged track – this can be rather muddy in wet weather. Descend to the road at the top end of **South Newington**. Cross over the road and walk down the high street into the village. (2 miles)

Date walk completed:

TUSMORE PARK AND THE VILLAGES

THE STREAM NEAR STOKE LYNE

Distance:
8 miles

Map: OS Explorer 191 – Banbury, Bicester & Chipping Norton

Starting point:
The church of St
Mary in Cottisford.
GR 587310

How to get there: *Cottisford is 7 miles north of Bicester.
Leave Bicester on the A4421 road going northwards. After
about 3¹/₂ miles turn left and follow the road signs into
Fringford, where you then aim towards Hethe. Now
continue along the country lanes into Cottisford. Turn left at
the cross roads and park with consideration by the roadside
near to the church.*

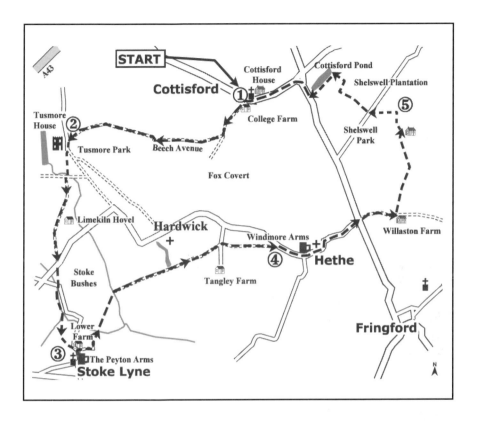

*A*n easy walk starting from the church of St Mary in the beautiful village of Cottisford – an adventure into Flora Thompson country. You have the opportunity of following her history before you walk through the superb Tusmore Park, to pass close to the famous large house. The route proceeds through a pleasing mixture of woodland and along the side of babbling streams on the approach to the lovely village of Stoke Lyne – your refreshment stop. You pass by the mounds of the original old village as you continue into pleasant countryside on the way to the attractive north Oxfordshire village of Hethe, where beautiful thatched cottages line the street. The route continues through Shelswell Park and passes the enchanting Cottisford Pool before returning to Cottisford village.

The Peyton Arms is a pretty country pub built in warm Cotswold stone and dating back to the 1800s. Originally called the Royal George the pub was renamed in the 1850s in honour of Sir Henry Peyton, who was then lord of the manor. The pub is a popular place with the locals, who like to swap stories and exchange gossip – the talking shop where spirits and glasses are lifted. Walkers are very welcome and will enjoy the beer served straight from the barrel – Hook Norton Best Bitter, Old Hookey Mild and seasonal ales. This is a traditional pub where home-cooked pub food and sandwiches are very popular and may be eaten in the small snug, the lounge or the large garden – you will share the garden with geese and rabbits – and there is a separate games/pool room.

> **You will enjoy** *a visit to this award-winning pub and it is easy to see why it is on the CAMRA National Inventory of classic pubs; this lists but 143 of the 60,000 pubs in the country.*
> *Telephone: 01869 345285; website: www.peytonarms.com;*
> *e-mail: info@peytonarms.com*

The Walk

① From the church, proceed up through **Cottisford**.

Cottisford is a tiny village which was founded in Saxon times. In 1066, William the Conqueror gave the manor of Cottisford to the Norman Baron Hugh de Grantmesnil as a reward for valiant services at the Battle of Hastings. Today, the village is renowned for its connection with Flora Thompson. Flora was born Flora Jane Thimms in 1876 at Watford Tunnel Cottage in the neighbouring hamlet of Juniper and spent most of her childhood

at 'The End House', which has since been renamed 'Larkrise Cottage'. She went to school in Cottisford. In 1900, the village comprised just 30 cottages and it was in her book Lark Rise to Candleford *that Flora recorded the standing joke about Cottisford: a traveller asked the way there only to be told that he had just walked right through it! Spare the time to visit the tiny church of St Mary the Virgin, where there is a plaque to the memory of Flora. You can obtain a copy of an interesting booklet entitled* Cottisford and its Church *as well as* Cottisford Revisited.

After about 150 yards, go left along the clear farm track passing by the building conversions of **College Farm**. Continue down the lovely wide track for about ¼ mile, then turn right and continue along a pleasant green track set to the left of the field hedge. This easy walking will soon bring you through a beautiful avenue of beech trees as you approach **Tusmore Park**. Bear right and then left to continue into the main park. Walk along a stone track to the left of more beech trees to arrive in the parkland, where superb, large deciduous trees can be enjoyed in their full splendour. The now green track arcs left towards the impressive building of **Tusmore House** and you will arrive on its driveway. (1½ miles)

In medieval times, Tusmore was a village but its population was wiped out by the Black Death around 1385. Sir Roger de Cottisford built the first Tusmore House and set it in a vast area of beautiful parkland. The present Tusmore House was built in recent years and is the fifth house on the site.

② Go left along the driveway passing to the left of the house. At the end of the main building, bear right onto a footpath that runs almost parallel with the large lake at the rear of the building. This path will take you through some hand-gates until you arrive on a tarmac estate lane. Go right and then left to

THE PEYTON ARMS, ONCE KNOWN AS THE ROYAL GEORGE PUB

continue into open countryside and onto another good track. Bear right onto the track that crosses a large cultivated field and you will see **Limekiln Hovel** to your left. The track bends left and you will soon arrive on a lane. Here, turn right and then left to enter **Stoke Bushes**. Proceed through the copse and you will arrive on another lane. Cross over this lane and go over the stile opposite. Cross the timber footbridge; then turn sharp left and walk by the side of the stream, aiming for another footbridge in the hedge ahead. Proceed up the pastureland and pass to the right of a farm cottage to a further stile. Now bear left and cross the next field to a farm gate by the side of **Thelma Cottage**. (1½ miles)

③ Proceed up the lane into the village of **Stoke Lyne** to the Peyton Arms pub.

Originally Stoke Lyne was called just Stoke, an Old English name meaning 'outlying farm'. Prior to the Norman Conquest the manor of Stoke was one of a number of estates held by Tostig, Earl of Northumbria, who died in 1066 in a battle against his brother King Harold. In 1416 the Lyne family became lords of the manor and the village became known as Stoke Lyne. The village is the setting for Flora Thompson's book Still Glides the Stream.

When you have had your refreshments, return down the lane and go right up the good track in front of **Lower Farm**. This track will lead you onto a lane going into the old village. The lane bends left and when at its bottom proceed on the footpath signed 'Hethe 1¾ miles'. As you enter the field of sheep you will see the remains of the old village to your right. Cross over the field and then the footbridge, which takes you into a large cultivated area. The clear footpath continues up the middle of the field and you bear right over a further footbridge onto a path that soon becomes a wide farm track set to the right of the field hedge. Proceed ahead through the hand-gate and through the small copse, then continue on a farm track that eventually reaches the driveway to **Tangley Farm**. Cross over the driveway and continue across the field opposite to the hedge corner. Now bear left and walk along the good farm track, which will soon take you to the right of the village allotments to reach the main road into the village of **Hethe**. (2¼ miles)

On the doorstep of Shelswell Park, the village of Hethe straggles across a lovely valley threaded by a willow-lined brook. There is a chapter in Flora Thompson's Lark Rise to Candleford *referring to the park, to Queen Victoria's Golden Jubilee celebrations and to* meeting the JP. Hethe is a charming village with a number of thatched cottages to admire. The name Hethe is generally understood to mean heathland. A ridge that runs by a small stream, marks the location of the first major dwelling, which was built in the 15th century. The church of St Edmund and St George is situated in the centre of the village of Hethe and is a picture in spring when the front of the churchyard is yellow with waving daffodils.

④ Go right along the road into the village. You will pass by the entrance to the village hall, the **Windmore Arms** pub and the church and will soon reach the village green and war memorial. Continue through this pleasant village and shortly you will arrive at the **Cottisford** road. Cross over the road and proceed down the driveway opposite towards **Willaston Farm**. Just before you reach the farm buildings, go left past a large oak tree and proceed over the stile by the farm gate. Cross the cultivated field and

continue ahead, descending to go through a hand-gate. The path now rises past more fine oaks and you will arrive on the driveway of **Shelswell House**. Cross the driveway and walk to the left of the field fence until you arrive at a small bridle-gate. (1½ miles)

⑤ Here turn left and cross over the parkland, aiming for a further large oak tree. Go through the hand-gate and cross over a lane. Walk along a fenced footpath by the side of the deciduous trees in **Shelswell Plantation**. At its end, go through the hand-gate and turn right to take the footpath around the edge of the next field. The path bends left and then left again for you to walk by the side of **Cottisford Pond**. You are likely to see ducks, coots and even Canada geese enjoying the freedom of this large pond before you reach the road at the end of some trees. Turn right up the road into the village of **Cottisford**. At the crossroads, near to some former estate houses, turn left and walk back to the church. (1¼ miles)

Date walk completed:

SALFORD AND THE COTSWOLD VILLAGES

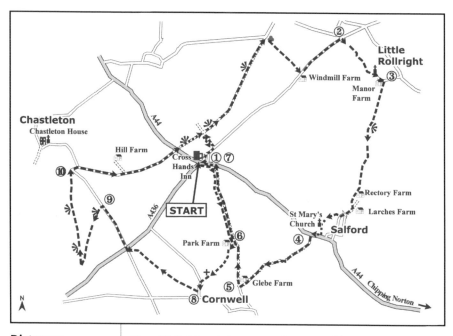

Distance:
12½ miles

Starting point:
The roadside at the rear of the Cross Hands Inn, Salford Hill. GR 270290

Map: OS Outdoor Leisure 45 – The Cotswolds

How to get there: *Salford Hill is some 24 miles north-west of Oxford. Leave Oxford on the A44 (the Woodstock road) and continue through Chipping Norton going towards Moreton-in-Marsh. After about 4 miles you will see the Cross Hands Inn at the junction with the A436 road.*

*T*his is a superb walk from the Cross Hands pub into attractive Cotswold countryside to enjoy super views of the surrounding landscape. The route takes you near to the famous Rollright Stones and then descends into Little Rollright village. Good paths and pleasing views can be enjoyed on the way into Salford village. You then have the option of detouring back to the pub for lunch before carrying on with the walk. You then follow lovely paths to a charming church on the edge of Cornwell. Stroll into the village and then up to the A436 road before walking a lovely ridge path towards Chastleton. Here the walk takes you along the front of a fine Jacobean house with its dovecote before you return to your car.

The Cross Hands Inn, set on the edge of the beautiful Cotswolds, is believed to be the highest public house in Oxfordshire. During the Second World War, the inn was visited by Winston Churchill when he reviewed the Royal Durham Regiment stationed at nearby Adlestrop. This 16th-century coaching inn has been a popular resting place for travellers for very many years and is a popular haunt of walkers in the area. There are panoramic views over the surrounding countryside and quality food is served at a reasonable price. If a ploughman's platter (ham, beef, Cheddar and Stilton) is your taste, then you can do no better, or perhaps you will fancy the Salford mixed grill to test your appetite. I prefer to eat out in the garden to watch the world go by but the Chastleton dining room is popular with many visitors. Local Hook Norton ale is on tap, as are Adnam's and Hancock's ales.

Telephone: *01608 643106; website: www.crosshandsinn.co.uk; e-mail: crosshandsinn@hotmail.com*

 *The Walk*

① Stroll through the small caravan park up to the country road at the rear of the inn, then continue up the grass verge for 200 yards. Now go left down a good farm track (walking in a north-westerly direction) – there is a pleasing view ahead of you. In about ¼ mile turn right along a well defined farm track. After about a mile of fine walking you approach a road and here bear right to continue along

CHASTLETON HOUSE

the track for 750 yards to arrive on a road. Head left along the side of this quiet country road for the next ¹/₂ mile towards a road junction. (2 miles)

If you can spare the time, stroll beyond the road junction to see the famous Rollright Stones. The legend of the stones tells us that the king and his army were marching through the Cotswolds when they came upon an old witch. She addressed the king saying, 'Seven long strides thou shalt take, and if Long Compton thou canst see then the King of England thou shalt be'. The king took the seven strides and on the seventh the ground rose up forming a long mound which blocked his view of the village. The witch then turned the king and the army into stone. The King Stone overlooks Long Compton, and his five knights, in a whispering group, overlook Little Rollright.

② Just before the junction, turn right into a cultivated field and descend the clear, wide farm track. After 300 yards bear right and then left to continue down the track where newly planted trees form an avenue – the village and church of **Little Rollright** are ahead of you. Descend past the church and walk along the village road. (¹/₂ mile)

It is such a pleasure to stroll through the rural community of Little Rollright. I am always intrigued by the gnarled tree stump in the village. Take time to visit the church of St Philip to see the very unusual stone-workings inside.

③ Just after passing the last building, head right following the fingerpost and walking to the right of the buildings of **Manor Farm**. Soon you will arrive at a cultivated field and walk to a stile at its top. Go over this and continue to the left of the field hedge, enjoying the fine view to your left before descending to a stile into woodland. Proceed through the trees, cross the stream and continue until you reach the road near to **Larches Farm**. Head right along the farm road into the village of **Salford**. At the road junction, bear right and just before **Chase Cottage** turn right over a stile into pastureland. Walk the well used path to the right of a wall, then bear left to enter the churchyard of **St Mary's church**,

THE CROSS HANDS INN, SAID TO BE THE HIGHEST PUB IN OXFORDSHIRE

passing to the left of the church. Exit via the church lychgate and follow the hedged path to the A44 road. Head right along the verge of the road for about 75 yards. (1³/₄ miles)

④ Cross over the A44 with care and proceed through a gateway onto a path/track that hugs the right-hand edge of the field. At the field corner, bear right onto a wide farm track that leads over attractive countryside passing to the left of **Glebe Farm** to reach a farm lane. (³/₄ mile)

⑤ Head right up the lane to **Park Farm**. (¹/₂ mile)

⑥ If you want to return to the **Cross Hands Inn** for lunch, you should carry on past **Park Farm** and then **Hollis Hill Farm** until you arrive back at the A44 (Moreton-in-Marsh to Oxford road). Turn left along the edge of the road to reach the **Cross Hands Inn**.

⑦ Retrace your steps, cross the busy A44 road and go left along the grass verge for about 30 yards. Now turn right down the lane towards **Cornwell**. Walk this good lane, which becomes a tarmac farm track, passing by **Hollis Hill Farm** to reach **Park Farm** again. (1¹/₄ miles)

Go along the entrance drive to Park Farm and then bear left over a stile following the waymarker

direction to a farm gate. Descend into a dell and then bear left to reach the field end. Head right over a footbridge and walk up the field to a track and reach a pathway by **St Peter's church** in **Cornwell**.

St Peter's church is part of the estate of the Hon. Peter Ward and his family, who live in the impressive Cornwell Manor, which was mentioned in **Domesday Book**. *It is believed that the original village of Cornwell was situated nearby and rebuilt in its current position after being wiped out during the time of the Black Death.*

Proceed through the churchyard and then bear left and stroll diagonally through the orchard in the grounds of **Cornwell Manor** to reach the road bend on the edge of the village. Head left down the road into the village, taking time to admire lovely Cotswold cottages with a stream running through their gardens. Descend to the bottom of the dell. (³/₄ mile)

⑧ Go right up a waymarked path and leave the village. This good path passes through a farm gate, ascending gently towards a second farm gate in the left-hand corner of the large field. Proceed up the farm track to the right of the field hedge and continue in a north-westerly direction up to woodland. A clear bridleway leads through the trees and you will soon arrive on a road near to a crossroads with the **A436**. Cross over the **A436** and proceed up the quiet country road opposite. Walk up the roadside edge for just under ¹/₂ mile looking out for a waymarked path set in the trees to your left. (1 mile)

⑨ Enter the trees, going over the stile to enter the woodland and reach a further stile at its end. Here you will arrive in the open once again. Take the path heading left (south-east). This well used path will lead you to the left of trees and after a further 200 yards you turn right into the woodland. Exit via the stile onto a good farm track and head right enjoying the fine view to your left. After almost 1 mile of delightful walking you will arrive at trees near to the road. Go over the stile and then bear left onto a good track along the top of **Peasewell Wood**. (1³/₄ miles)

⑩ At the end of **Peasewell Wood,** turn right and proceed down an avenue of trees to reach the road near to **Chastleton House**. Head right along the road to enjoy a fine view of the front of the National Trust house and its church.

Have your camera ready for a photo opportunity as you pass the fine gates of the superb Jacobean mansion of Chastleton House, which stands on land once owned by Robert Catesby, who took part in the Gunpowder Plot. Designed by Sir John Vanbrugh, this magnificent mansion was built on land given by Queen Anne to John, 1st Duke of Marlborough in 1705.

Proceed along the road for about 600 yards past the NT car park to the road corner. Bear left over the cattle grid and walk along the quiet road into open countryside. This leads past the entrance to **Hill Farm** and affords a typical Cotswold view. After nearly a mile of delightful walking you will arrive at the **A44** road. Cross over and continue up the farm track opposite for a further 500 yards. At the junction of tracks, turn right to arrive back on the road near to the **Cross Hands Inn**. Here turn right to return to your parked car. (2¹/₄ miles)

Date walk completed:

SOMERTON & THE HEYFORDS

THE OXFORD CANAL NEAR STEEPLE ASTON

Distance:
8 miles

Map: OS Explorer 191 – Banbury, Bicester & Chipping Norton

Starting point:
St James's church in
Somerton.
GR 497286

How to get there: *Somerton is 16 ¹/₂ miles north of Oxford. It is best approached from Junction 10 of the M40 along the A430 (the Ardley road). After about ¹/₂ mile, go right through Fewcott along the Somerton road to reach the village.*

*F*rom the peaceful village of Somerton this gentle walk takes you over the Oxford Canal and up country tracks into the attractive villages of Middle Aston and Steeple Aston, where there are many fine stone houses to admire. From Steeple Aston, the route follows lovely paths down into typical Oxfordshire countryside, passing near to the 'eyecatcher' which was built to the east of Steeple Aston as a feature of landscape for nearby Rousham House. After crossing over the mainline railway you reach the Oxford Canal once again and walk along its towpath into the quiet village of Lower Heyford. The route continues along the canal bank into Upper Heyford – a village that was famous as an airbase during the two world wars and later became a USAF base.

The Bell Inn was originally built in the 18th century as a Wesleyan chapel and was converted into two cottages before it became the attractive inn you see today. Being situated near to the Oxford Canal means that many narrowboat owners are regular customers and the inn offers a good mix of foods. From baguettes to lasagne to steak – there is something on the menu board to suit everyone. The Bell is open from 11.30 am to 3 pm and from 6 pm to 11 pm each day (10.30 pm on Sunday) and food is available at any time during these periods. You can expect a good selection of real ale because the locals choose the ales to be on tap on a regular basis – three are offered at the weekend. In the summer, it is very pleasant to eat and sup a pint of the best real ale in the large garden.

Telephone: *01869 347176*

 *The Walk*

① Stroll down the footpath near the entrance gate to **St James's church**. Just before reaching the road, bear right to continue along a good hedged track going generally west. Soon you will arrive in pastureland and should continue following the direction of the waymarkers. As you progress over several fields the footpath arcs gently south-west and you will see the village of **North Aston** up to your right. Eventually you arrive at a gate onto a stone farm track near to the mainline railway. Bear right and cross over the railway line, then proceed over

33

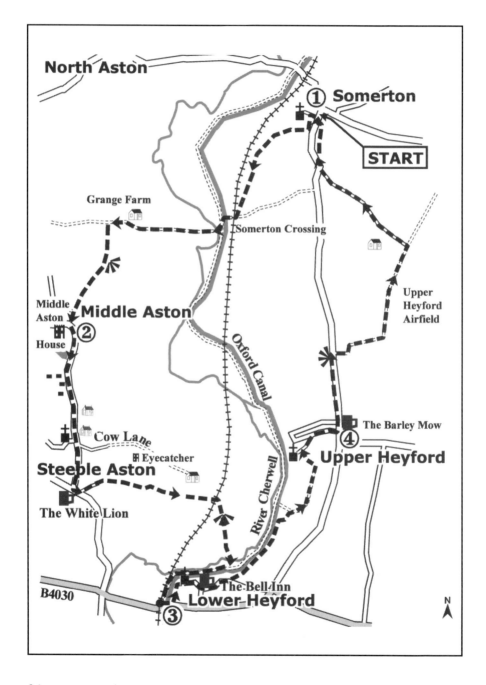

the **Oxford Canal** – the track soon becomes a hedged footpath/track. As you emerge from the hedged path, **Grange Farm** is to your right ahead. Walk up the field past the farm, going through the hand-gate onto the farm drive. After about 100 yards, you will reach some trees and a hedge. Here, go left and walk the **Cherwell Walk** path set to the right of the hedge, following the waymarker direction. In just over 1/2 mile you will be approaching the village of **Middle Aston** on a footpath set to the left of a wall and you emerge on the road near to **Middle Aston House**. (2 miles)

Middle Aston House is a technical

training college set back from the road amid trees.

② Head left along the road past the fine house and continue past the poultry farm and industrial estate. Soon you will be descending into **Steeple Aston,** where you pass by the village hall and the pre school building and then the parish church. This is a lovely village and you will enjoy seeing the very attractive stone houses before you reach the road near to the **White Lion** pub. Go left along the quiet road for about 50 yards.

Steeple Aston is a delightful village of stone houses and

ONCE A WESLEYAN CHAPEL, THE BELL IS NOW AN ATTRACTIVE VILLAGE INN

cottages – it was established as a market town of some 200 souls according to **Domesday Book.** *Probably the most famous resident was Judge Page, the 'Hanging Judge'. There is an alabaster effigy of Sir Francis Page in the parish church revealing that he was made King's Sergeant at Law in 1715. In 1726 he became Judge of the Common Pleas and the next year was appointed Senior Judge of the King's Bench.*

Bear left down a lane called **The Dickridge**. After passing some cottages, you arrive on a concrete farm lane by a fingerpost which says 'Lower Heyford 2'. Continue through two kissing gates and a hand-gate to reach a small area of woodland where, to your left, you will see the 'eyecatcher' for **Rousham House**. Continue in this direction; go over a stile, then walk through a narrow tree plantation. A further stile takes you back into pastureland and you descend to reach and cross the bridge over the mainline railway. Bear right immediately after crossing the bridge and diagonally cross pastureland. Go over the stile at the field corner and proceed along the tree-lined path through a pleasant area beside the **River Cherwell**. Cross over the river bridge onto the towpath of the **Oxford Canal** and head right, walking in a westerly direction. You will find a number of colourful narrowboats moored on

the canal and after about 200 yards you can take a short-cut over a canal bridge to arrive in the centre of **Lower Heyford** village near to the Bell Inn. The full route continues along the towpath, which arcs left and passes **Lower Heyford Wharf** to reach the B4030 main road near to **Heyford station**. (2¹/₄ miles)

③ Go left over the stone bridge set immediately before the main road and ascend to pass the entrance to **Lower Heyford Wharf**. After some 20 yards, turn left through a kissing gate and proceed along a good footpath past the recreation area. You will pass to the right of the wharf. Just before you reach the canal, bear right, proceed through a hand-gate and walk along the short hedged path to arrive on the road near to **St Mary's church**. Continue along the road and soon you will arrive in the centre of **Lower Heyford** by the **Bell Inn**.

Until the 13th century it was known as just Heyford and it was not until the 15th century that the name Lower Heyford appeared. Today, it is a peaceful village set back from the main road with the Oxford Canal (which was opened in 1790 to transport coal to the Midlands) at its rear.

From the pub, head left along the main road into the village where a number of thatched buildings will catch the eye. Bear left down **Mill Lane** and then turn right to go up past the sports area onto a waymarked footpath. This pleasant footpath will take you along the bank of the canal, which you can see through gaps in the trees. After some 250 yards, the path passes to the right of a new sewage works to reach a concrete lane. Turn right up this lane towards **Upper Heyford** to arrive on a lane just above **St Mary's church**. Bear right and follow the lane across the village green into the centre of the village, then walk up the side of the road to reach the main road. (2 miles)

④ Turn left along the pavement of the main road, passing the **Barley Mow** and a row of houses. Continue up the grass verge for some 300 yards beyond the last house and then cross over the road and proceed to the right, up the waymarked bridle-path. This path will lead you to the wire fence of **Upper Heyford airfield**.

Upper Heyford served as a First World War airbase between 1916 and 1920 and was a famous bomber station from 1927. It was leased to the USAF in 1951 and was occupied by them until 1994. Today, the base is largely unoccupied, with parts used for industrial purposes.

Walk round the perimeter fence in a clockwise direction for about 3/4 mile and arrive at a tarmac farm lane. Turn left along this lane. There are pleasant views all around and soon you will pass by a row of country cottages before you arrive at the main road once again. Turn right along the side of the road. Ignore the waymarked track to the right but go over the stile onto the waymarked footpath, which will lead you directly towards the village of **Somerton**. After crossing over pastureland/common land, you will arrive at a pair of stiles on the edge of the village. Go over these, pass some houses, and then take the first left-hand lane to arrive back on the main road. Turn right and continue along the road for 50 yards, then turn left down **Church Street** to arrive back at the village church where your walk started. (1 3/4 miles)

Date walk completed:

CHARLBURY
AND THE
EVENLODE VALLEY

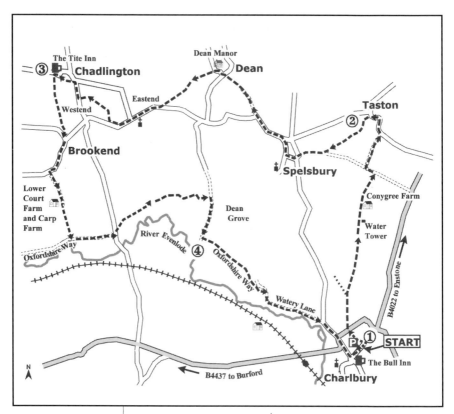

Distance:	Maps: OS Explorer 180 – Oxford, Witney & Woodstock and 191 –
9 miles	Banbury, Bicester & Chipping Norton

Starting point:
Public car park at the Spendlove Centre in Charlbury. GR 358197

How to get there: *Charlbury is 8 miles north of Witney. Approach the town on the B4022 (the Witney road). The Spendlove Centre car park is on the left as you enter the town.*

WALK 6

*T*his delightful walk around the beautiful villages of Middle Oxfordshire starts from the small town of Charlbury and passes through undulating countryside up to the hamlet of Taston before progressing into Spelsbury, where thatched cottages catch your eye. The route passes close to a fine manor house at Dean and then crosses pastureland into Chadlington, where refreshment awaits at the Tite Inn. The way takes you through St Nicholas's churchyard and over cultivated fields to the village of Brookend. A stroll up the main street leads you past a carp farm and soon you will be able to join the Oxfordshire Way near to the River Evenlode. Good footpaths and tracks take you over attractive rolling countryside back to Charlbury to explore its peaceful, historic centre.

The Tite Inn, a handsome 17th-century hostelry, affords a superb view over an Area of Outstanding Natural Beauty. The lovely garden contains mature shrubs and trees and offers an ideal environment to relax and to sup one of the award winning beers – Tite Inn Bitter, Young's Brewery Bitter, Daniel's Hammer or Kangaboo. The Tite has had hundreds of beers over the last 15 years and on the website you will find a list of these under the title 'Beers that we have had'. Apart from the superb draught beers, excellent fresh food is a big attraction. You may eat in the bar area, in the garden or perhaps indulge yourself in the informal restaurant and garden room – this is covered with a vine in the summer. All the food is cooked on the premises using only the freshest produce, including local vegetables and game when in season.

The inn is open *from Tuesday to Sunday each week between 12 noon and 2.30 pm and in the evenings from 6.30 pm to 11 pm. It is closed on Mondays except for bank holiday lunchtimes. Children and dogs under control are allowed in the inn.*
Telephone: 01608 676475; website: www.titeinn.com.
e-mail: willis@titeinn.com

The Walk

① From the **Spendlove Centre** car park exit onto the road and go left for about 50 yards. Now turn left up a hedged footpath that leads past the village recreation area to the B4437 road. Cross this road and go over the stile opposite, following the fingerpost signed 'Taston 1¼'. Initially the path descends into trees, then you cross a footbridge over a

THE MEMORIAL IN TASTON

stream and ascend to a field stile. At the next stile you bear right and aim for the far left-hand corner of the large field. After passing through the hedge, bear left over the stile and follow the path initially set to the left of the field hedge. Soon you will be walking on a farm track across a large cultivated area and should aim for a water tower at the field end, then pass to the left of **Conygree Farm**. Continue until you are walking to the right of a field hedge, maintaining a north-east direction, and then emerge through a gap in the hedge onto a farm track. Head left along the track past **Coathouse Farm**; the track arcs right to reach the road in the hamlet of **Taston**. Turn left and continue up the road until you reach the remains of an ancient village cross. (1½ miles)

Taston is a very small hamlet with a tiny green. The old wayside stone cross, which has given the hamlet its name, is called the Thor Stone after the northern god of thunder.

② Head left along the good track/lane signed 'Spelsbury ½' and follow the clear waymarkers. Descend into trees and bushes and cross over a couple of small footbridges, still following the waymarker direction. Soon you pass through a hand-gate onto a lane in the village of **Spelsbury**. At the road, turn right into the village, taking time to admire the thatched cottages which line the road.

Spelsbury is charming but all that remains of the old village are a few thatched cottages, a row of gabled almshouses and All Saints' church. In the churchyard lie the unknown graves of three Earls of Rochester, one of them a notorious and dissolute poet. The first earl was closely associated with King Charles during the Civil War and he commanded the left wing at Edgehill. The second earl, a brilliant poet whose scurrilous wit spared neither king nor court, was called to the House of Lords at the age of 20. It was he who pinned to the king's bedroom door these lines:

*'Here lies our sovereign lord the king;
Whose word no man relies on;
He never says a foolish thing
Nor ever does a wise one.'*

The third earl was his son, who survived him by just two years.

The road arcs right and then left as you leave the village on the quiet Chadlington road. Where the road bends sharp left, proceed ahead onto a bridleway path signed 'Dean ¹/₂'. The path heads north-west; at the junction of bridleways, bear left, going over footbridges and then ascending pastureland to the road in

the hamlet of **Dean**. Cross over this road and bear left and then right to progress through the hamlet along a road that curves to the left in front of **Dean Manor**. At the next bend, go left onto the bridle-path signed 'Chadlington ¹/₂' and walk into **Chadlington**. The route descends over a footbridge and then takes you along the top of pastureland where you can enjoy a pleasant view to your left. Soon you will arrive on the road at **Eastend** in **Chadlington**. Turn right and head up the road into the village. You will pass by the **church of St Nicholas** and then **Chadlington House**. Shortly after passing **Church Road**, bear right through a kissing gate into the playing fields and walk along the path by the side of the Cotswold stone wall to a second kissing gate. Do not go through the gate but head to the right up the edge of the playing field and past the pavilion to a further gate in the top left-hand corner of the field. Go through this gate and bear left to go through a gap in the hedge onto a footpath, aiming towards some residential properties. The route goes via a fenced path onto the road. Turn right and walk on the pavement until you reach the junction with the other end of **Church Road**. Here, go left over a stile and across some common land. Now turn right and proceed over a corner stile into a private garden. Proceed through the garden and exit over a stone stile onto a footpath, bearing right to emerge on the road opposite the **Tite Inn**, where your lunch awaits. (3 miles)

③ From the **Tite Inn,** turn right and go down the road for 40 yards, then turn left onto a clear signed footpath – 'Brookend $\frac{1}{2}$'. You will be walking in a generally southward direction on a good path that arcs gently left until you reach a road in **Brookend**. Turn left at the road and stroll through this delightful hamlet, bearing right at the main road. After about 200 yards, turn left up the driveway to **Lower Court Farm** and

a carp farm. Pass to the left of the buildings and continue on a bridle-path set to the right of the field hedge. You pass through a farm gate and ahead of you is a pleasing view over the **Evenlode Valley** and rolling Oxfordshire countryside. After about 300 yards, you will reach a junction of tracks. Head left along the **Oxfordshire Way**. After 600 yards cross over **Catsham Lane** to continue past **Little Wood** and **Greenhill** copses. The wide track descends towards trees and you pass through a hand-gate, bearing right then left to continue along the **Oxfordshire Way** until you reach a

THE TITE INN IS A HANDSOME 17TH-CENTURY PUB

farm track. Turn right down this track, passing through a farm gate, then walking to the right of **Dean Grove**. (2³/₄ miles)

④ At the end of the trees, look out for, and go left over, a stile into pastureland. Follow the line of the well-walked path going south-east, to cross a footbridge. Continue up the left edge of the field. A couple of kissing gates lead you to a bend in the field hedge where you exit and turn right down **Water Lane** – a good track that leads to the **Spelsbury** road in **Charlbury**.

Sited on a hillside, Charlbury looks across the Evenlode Valley to the glory of Wychwood Forest. The settlement originated as a fortified Saxon camp. Its Norman church is by tradition associated with Saint Diuma, the first Bishop of Mercia, who died in 658. The vicarage was the birthplace in 1624 of Anne Downer, who married a Quaker and was the first woman to preach in London. Charlbury became a stronghold for the Quakers and the Friends' Meeting House was built in 1779.

In 1853 the Oxford, Worcester, Wolverhampton railway was opened and Charlbury railway station, which was designed by Isambard Kingdom Brunel, remains a major link with Oxford, London and Evesham.

Turn right and head up the road into **Charlbury**. You will pass by Armada House and the Quaker House and will soon arrive in the middle of the small town. Turn left up the A4022 (the Witney road) to find the Spendlove Centre car park. (1³/₄ miles)

Date walk completed:

THE BLENHEIM PARK WALK

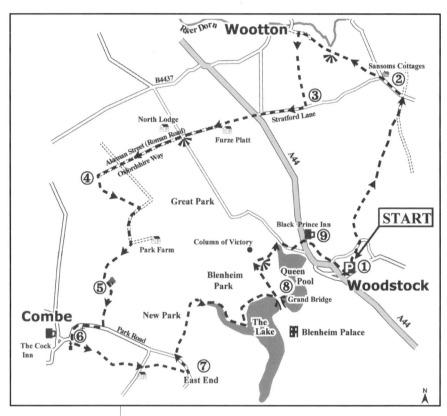

Distance:
9¹/₂ miles

Starting point:
Hensington Road
car park in
Woodstock.
GR 446168

Map: OS Explorer 180 – Oxford, Witney & Woodstock

How to get there: *Woodstock is 7¹/₂ miles north-west of Oxford on the A44. Hensington Road is to the right as you enter the village from the south.*

*T*his fine walk in the park starts from the delightful village of Woodstock where honey-coloured stone antique shops line the main street. Initially, you head towards Wootton then you veer across the A44 road into the magnificent Blenheim Park, where the landmark Column of Victory stands so proud. Superb trees catch the eye as you pass through the western part of the park on the way to Combe, where the Cock Inn provides a warm welcome to walkers. Lovely paths take you into East End and then you re-enter the park walking by the lake to reach the Grand Bridge and a superb view of the famous palace. You emerge from the park near to the Black Prince Inn and can then stroll by a lovely stream.

The Cock Inn – there can be few better places to sit than in the garden of this hostelry, supping a pint of real ale. It is a traditional Cotswold pub serving award-winning cask ales with superb fare – a true family inn, with roaring log fires which bring to life traditional furniture under exposed beams. In the family tradition of 'The best takes a little longer' you will find that the landlady cooks everything to order, so there might be a short delay while meals are beautifully prepared and presented using fresh, local produce.

From Tuesday to Friday, food is available between 12 noon and 2.30 pm and in the evening between 6 pm and 8.30 pm (8.45 pm on Friday); on Monday, lunch is served between 12 noon and 2.30 pm; Saturday 12 noon to 4 pm and 6 pm to 8.45 pm; Sunday lunch is from 12 noon to 3 pm – booking required. No food is served on Sunday or Monday evenings.

Set in the delightful village of Combe, overlooking the village green, the busy bar is a treat and you can join in with local people trading stories and banter in this friendly inn. If you would like to know more about the care taken in looking after your cask ales or your wines please do not hesitate to ask the landlord who will be delighted to show you around the cellar.

Telephone: *01993 891 288; website: www.thecockinn.cotswoldinns.com e-mail: info@thecockinn.cotswoldinns.com*

THE CHURCH OF ST LAWRENCE IN COMBE

 *The Walk*

① Leave the **Hensington Road** car park at its rear and proceed to the right along the backs of houses to reach a road junction. Turn right up the tarmac lane behind more houses, past the **Woodstock cemetery**. Where you pass by the sewage works, the lane becomes a hedged path and you continue up this. After about 1 mile of pleasant walking, go through a gate onto the **B4027** road and head left along its grass verge until you reach the cross-

roads by **Sansoms Cottages**. (1¹/₂ miles)

② Here, go left through a kissing gate on the corner and walk along the clear path going over a cultivated field to reach and go through a hand-gate. Bear right to go through a further gate, then turn left over a footbridge and you will reach another gate onto open land. Enjoy the pleasant valley view to the right, embracing a pond and the **River Dorn** below with the village of **Wootton** on the hill opposite. Bear left through a garden onto a wide track at a junction of paths.

Cross over the track and proceed on a footpath set to the right of the field hedge. Maintain this direction over three fields – you will be treated to a fine display of wild poppies in the summer months – and go over a couple of stiles to reach **Stratford Lane**; it follows the course of an old Roman road and is also part of the **Oxfordshire Way**. (³/₄ mile)

③ Turn right along the lane up to a junction of roads, where you go left to reach the A44 road. Cross the road with care and proceed through the gate opposite, then continue along the **Oxfordshire Way**, passing through a second gate onto a farm track. Go right, then left, over a stile onto a clear path, maintaining your direction – aim for a stile to the right of **Furze Platt**. A second stile and a farm gate allow you to stride out along the **Oxfordshire Way** and soon you are walking on a good, wide, green track called **Akeman Street** – an old Roman road. Follow this lovely track until you cross over a farm lane and then descend into trees to reach another track. (1³/₄ miles)

THE COCK INN IS A TRADITIONAL COTSWOLD PUB

④ Turn right along the tree-lined track and then, after about 150 yards, bear left over a footbridge and take a clear path across cultivated land, heading for trees. Turn right along the track that hugs the trees and soon you will arrive on another farm track with **Park Farm** to your left. Here, bear right onto a footpath that leads back into woodland, descending into a small valley then proceeding ahead up the pathway that arcs left up to a main track. Turn left and then right on a waymarked path that leads to a 'step' stile over the Cotswold stone wall. (1 mile)

⑤ Go over the stile, turn left and then right, and walk on the clear footpath set to the left of the field hedge until you reach **Park Road** on the edge of **Combe**. Turn right along the road past the attractive thatched property called **Whittons** and the **Methodist church**. You can either continue along the side of the quiet road as it arcs left into the centre of the village or, perhaps, enter the fine recreation ground, cutting the corner to reach the village green opposite the **Cock Inn**. (1 mile)

⑥ From the green walk up the waymarked footpath (signed 'East End 1½ miles') and enter the churchyard of **St Lawrence's church**. The route proceeds through the churchyard which you exit at its rear via a fascinating gateway made of gravestones. The path curves to the right into the trees, and you bear left along a clear footpath that crosses a cultivated field and then hugs the side of woodland – in spring you will enjoy glimpses of bluebells in the woods. The path then veers right to reach a lane (**Bolton's Lane**). Cross the lane and continue eastwards over pastureland, negotiating three stiles to reach **Park Road** near to **Blenheim Palace's High Park**. (³/₄ mile)

⑦ Head left along the road until you reach the rear entrance to **Blenheim Park**. Go right through the gateway into the park and then bear left along the tarmac road. After almost ¹/₂ mile of walking in very attractive surroundings you will see a fence ahead of you with an intriguing sign, 'SLOW PHEASANTS CROSSING'. Just before reaching the sign, turn right along a clear footpath that arcs left and go over a stile in the fence. Turn right and stroll along the delightful path by the side of the lake, where grebes, seagulls, coots, ducks, swans and moorhens may be at play – this is a pretty picture indeed. As you continue along the beech tree-lined track above the lake, a fine view of **Blenheim Palace** unfolds to the right over the waters.

Sir John Vanbrugh's grandiose masterpiece was built for John

Churchill, 1st Duke of Marlborough, and many famous craftsmen were involved with its construction and ornate decoration. Capability Brown created the truly magnificent Blenheim Park with its very fine lake. The house was a gift from a grateful nation after the Duke's victory over the French and Bavarians at Blenheim in 1704. Today, one of its main attractions is the room where Sir Winston Churchill was born in 1874 – he was the grandson of the 7th Duke of Marlborough. Sir Winston and his parents, Lord and Lady Randolph Churchill, are buried in the churchyard of the nearby village of Bladon.

Soon after passing a clump of trees circled by fencing, you will arrive by the **Grand Bridge** and can stroll onto this for an even better view of the magnificent palace. (1 mile)

⑧ Retrace your steps along the track and now bear right of the tree enclosure, ascending to a junction of tracks. At the junction, go right and continue the ascent. The path takes you near to the superb **Column of Victory** for an even better view over

Blenheim Palace before descending right once again to arrive on a park road near to the end of **Queen Pool**, from where there is a superb view looking towards the palace. At the junction of park roads, head right up the road to the north of **Queen Pool**, then bear left, leaving the tarmac road by going onto a path that leads to a gate set to the left of a cottage with a conservatory. Proceed through the gate to pass between houses to reach the **A44** road in **Woodstock**. (³/₄ mile)

⑨ Turn right and walk past the **Black Prince Inn** and then go left over a footbridge onto a clear footpath to the right of a stream.

Although there has been modern development in Woodstock, it still retains much of its 18th-century elegance. It is a pleasant village to stroll around and has a number of antique shops to visit.

Continue on the path as it bears right over a second footbridge and proceed through a gate onto a lane. Head left up the lane for some 325 yards to a junction then turn right to **Hensington Road** car park on the left. (1 mile)

Date walk completed:

OTMOOR OUTING

THE RIVER RAY NEAR THE WEIR

Distance:
6¹/₄ or 9³/₄ miles

Starting point:
The village green in
Oddington.
GR 553149

Map: OS Explorer 180 – Oxford, Witney & Woodstock

How to get there: Oddington is 9¹/₂ miles north of
Oxford. Leave Oxford on the B4027 road and follow the
Oddington signs from Islip.

*O*tmoor means 'fen of Otta' and the area is a curious one of marshland that has often been described as the 'forgotten land'. Criss-crossed by small streams, the flat moorland is liable to flooding. During the Second World War, it was used as a practice bombing ground by the RAF, with the result that it became an unlikely target for German bombers. Today, drainage systems have been introduced and water disposal is under control. The regular flooding of properties has become a thing of the past and in springtime the streams attract a variety of butterflies and insects. Wild flowers abound along the path edges with the result that the area has been bought by the RSPB, who have restored much of the wetland to encourage birds back to the area. This easy walk offers an opportunity to adventure into the forgotten land and to visit Islip and Oddington – two of Otmoor's 'seven towns'.

The Swan Inn is an ancient one, built in 1647, just two years after the Civil War skirmish at nearby Islip Bridge. Occupied as a tavern/coaching inn and a pub for most of its life, there is an olde worlde character to the building, with timber roof beams and a log fire producing a warm, welcoming atmosphere. Opening hours are 12 noon to 3 pm and 6 pm to 11 pm (10.30 pm on Sunday) and food is available at any of these times. The real ales are Greene King's Abbot Ale and IPA and it is very pleasant to sup a pint and enjoy a curry in the attractive garden at the rear. You may wish for a scrumptious baguette from the 'Lite Bite' menu or stay for a substantial meal from the main menu, on which you will find some 32 dishes ranging from steak and grills to curry.

Telephone: *01865 372590*

 *The Walk*

A visit to peaceful Oddington is like stepping back in time, although two village greens, some old farmhouses and the beautiful church of St Andrew are the only historic features that remain. The church is fascinating and the entrance key can be obtained from one of the neighbouring cottages. The village attracts many New Zealand visitors because the church contains a grave and memorial to a Maori princess. If you lift the rug in front of the

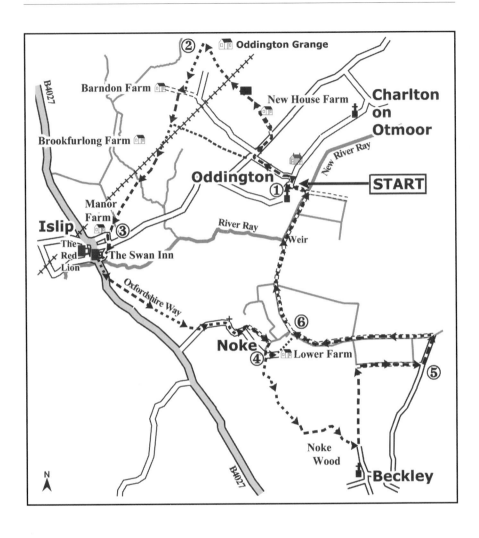

altar you will find an amazing
15th century memorial brass
depicting Ralph Hamsterley
(1499–1507), a former rector.
Intended to express the spiritual
humility of the deceased, the
rector is presented in his shroud
with maggots emerging from his

anatomy – a rather macabre
picture.

① From the village green, head up
the **Charlton-on-Otmoor** road, then
go left on the quiet lane to the
main road. Turn right up the grass
verge of the road. After 350 yards,

cross over the road and turn left onto the waymarked driveway towards **New House Farm**. The stone track becomes a footpath as you bear left of the farm complex and keep to the left of the field hedge over two large fields. Proceed past the derelict barn to the right of the second field – this was the original New House Farm – and proceed over the next field, aiming for a white kissing gate that leads over the railway line. Maintain your walking line and pass over the driveway to **Oddington Grange**, now a large farm. Cross over two small, fenced stretches of pastureland. At the second fence there is a stile, which carries a waymark for the **Oxfordshire Way**. (1¹/₂ miles)

② Turn about to the left here and walk on the Oxfordshire Way, going generally south-west, into **Islip**. Initially, the path goes over a footbridge, then you aim for the far right-hand corner of the next large field. A couple of stiles lead you alongside the next field hedge to reach the driveway to **Barndon Farm**. Head to the right along the driveway for 75 yards, then go left along a clear, wide, grass farm track. In just over ¹/₄ mile pass through the gap in the hedge and walk along the signed footpath on the other side of the hedge until you reach a stile into trees by the side of the railway line. Proceed over the railway line and cross a large cultivated field. After crossing a couple of footbridges you will be approaching the village of **Islip**, aiming for the far left corner of the final field. Here, a metal kissing gate allows you onto the road at the corner of **North Street**; there

THE 17TH-CENTURY SWAN INN

is a waymarker by the kissing gate – 'Wendlebury 4'. (1¹/₂ miles)

In Domesday Book, Islip was known as etelape – a name thought to relate to the River Ray, which was formerly called Ight or Gight. It was in this historic village that Edward the Confessor was born in about 1004. A painting of him in the church reminds us that Islip was his village and that he gave it to the monks of Westminster. Under the portrait are a few words from his will: 'I have given to Christ and to St Peter in Westminster the little town of Islippe wherein I was born.'

③ Head left along the street and continue into **Lower Street**, where you will find the **Swan Inn** by the **Islip Bridge**. When you are refreshed, proceed over the bridge across the **River Ray** and stroll up the side of the road for about 200 yards. Go left over a hedge stile and take the **Oxfordshire Way** footpath, which arcs gently left (south-east). Maintain this direction for 1 mile. You will go over a number of stiles and pass through a few metal kissing gates and eventually go over a stile into trees. Take the well used footpath into the village of **Noke**.

The small Anglo-Saxon village of Noke (the name means 'place at the oak') is situated on the

southern rim of Otmoor. Legend has it that the ghost of Benedict Winchcombe, who died in 1623, murdered by poachers on his own land, haunts the village of Noke. Benedict lived in the manor house and was known in his latter years as 'Old Winchcombe'. He was a very keen huntsman and locals who wish to retain the legend may tell you that the sound of horses and hounds can still be heard around the village. Benedict Winchcombe is buried in St Giles' churchyard and his memorial reads:

*'We know thou art not lost but sent before
Thy friends all left thy absence to deplore.
Nor can thy Virtues ever be forgotten
Tho in thy grave thy corpse be dead and rotten.
For ill tongued Envy to the World must tell
That as thou livdst thou didst and that was well.'*

Proceed down the main street in the small village taking time to admire the lovely **church of St Giles**. The road bends left and then right. Turn left in front of the pair of thatched cottages and then right onto a signed footpath (a green farm track) that runs along the back of houses. After passing a tennis hard-court the path curves right and you arrive by a small bridge on the

lane near to **Lower Farm**.
(1³/₄ miles)
    **Here is the point where you
have a choice of the shorter walk
or the longer option.**
    To complete the shorter route,
pass to the left of **Lower Farm** and
to the right of an attractive small
lake to reach a junction of tracks.
Here go left following the walk
description from point **6** below.

④ **To complete the longer walk,**
proceed across the lane and follow
the **Oxfordshire Way** waymarkers.
The route follows a hedged/fenced
footpath that circles around the field
curving left along the bottom of
Noke Wood. The path then takes
you up through the trees, ascending
gently into the open countryside to
the north-west of **Beckley**. After
300 yards, leave the **Oxfordshire
Way** by going left (north) and
descending a hedged footpath. After
about 500 yards of pleasant walking
bear right and pass through the field
hedge, pausing to enjoy the view up
to the right towards **Beckley** village.
Descend by the hedge to the field
corner and then head right along a
good track by a ditch where water
reeds and bulrush plants attract the
wildlife. Proceed in this direction
(east) over three fields and a couple
of footbridges until you reach a
lane. (2¹/₄ miles)

⑤ Go left along the lane for about
¹/₄ mile. Now head left along a

good, wide bridle-path going west.
To your left there is a hedge and
beyond this an old moat area. To
the right is the **Otmoor Nature
Reserve**. After about 1 mile of easy
walking you will reach an Otmoor
Nature Reserve sign. (1¹/₄ miles)

*Today, a large part of Otmoor is
protected as a sanctuary for wild
birds, and it is as peaceful and
secluded now as it was hundreds
of years ago. Birds have returned
in large numbers and you may be
lucky enough to see bittern, little
bittern, black tern, white stork,
black stork or purple heron.*

⑥ Continue along the wide bridle-
path, walking to the right of the
stream and curving northwards.
Soon the stream disappears beneath
the hedge but you continue along
the bridle-path still going
northwards. After crossing a bridge
over the **River Ray** continue ahead
with the **New River Ray** behind the
hedge – covered with blackberries in
autumn – to your left and the
church in **Charlton-on-Otmoor**
ahead on the horizon. Walk for 700
yards after crossing over the **River
Ray**, then head left up the stone
track to arrive back in the village of
Oddington. (1¹/₂ miles)

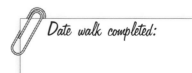
Date walk completed:

Walk 9

BURFORD AND THE NORTH COTSWOLD VILLAGES

DEER IN THE FIELDS NEAR STURT FARM AND STUD

Distance:
10¹/₂ miles

Starting point:
Public car park in
Burford.
GR 254123

Map: Outdoor Leisure 45 – The Cotswolds

How to get there: *Burford is 19 miles west of Oxford,
being situated 7¹/₂ miles west of Witney just off the A40
(Witney to Cheltenham road).*

*T*his fine walk in the North Cotswolds starts from picturesque Burford, where honey-coloured stone buildings line the high street and ducks, geese and swans add interest to the lovely River Windrush. The route leaves the car park by the river, passing the beautiful church, then crossing over the river into the attractive village of Fulbrook. As you progress into the Cotswold countryside, a good track takes you through a beautiful copse and past Faws Grove to a bit of Oxfordshire's Peak District – the walk down Dean Bottom to the church of St Oswald and Swinbrook village is a delight. A riverside path leads into Asthall for lunch and then through a stud farm where you are likely to see deer, pigs and cattle. After skirting the edge of Widford village, a pleasing riverside walk completes a day of adventure and delight.

The Maytime Inn is centuries old and quite delightful. It stands proudly in the centre of the ancient village of Asthall completing an inviting scene.

It is difficult to believe that in the early 1970s the building was condemned and closed down. Fortunately, it was saved and over the years it has been systematically transformed into a warm, welcoming inn with flagstone floors and log fires – a joy to visit.

You will be assured of good food at the inn and can choose from either the light meals or the à la carte menus, featuring vegetarian dishes and a special 'Little People's' menu. Daily selections, lunch and dinner, are displayed on a board in the bar.

They have a saying at the inn: 'Remember; when in the Cotswolds, eat well, drink merrily and sleep peacefully at the Maytime Inn, Asthall'.

Telephone: *01993 822068; fax: 01993 822635; website: www.themaytime.com*

 *The Walk*

The picturesque town of Burford has a superb, wide high street that sweeps down towards the

River Windrush and an ancient three-arched bridge. The high street contains all manner of beautiful old Cotswold houses, shops and inns dating from the 14th to the 17th century. This was once a great wool town and near

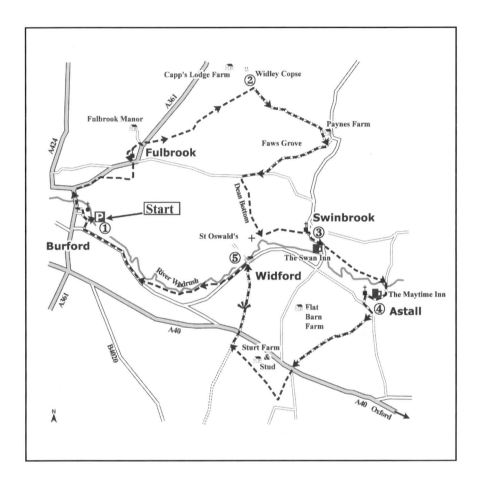

the middle of the high street is the 'Tolsey', where wealthy wool merchants held their meetings and collected tolls – now it houses a museum. In May 1649, at the end of the English Civil War, 340 of the Levellers were rounded up by Cromwell and his men and imprisoned in Burford church – carvings made by the incarcerated soldiers and the bullet holes of three executed ring leaders can still be seen.

① Stroll along **Church Lane** towards the town but bear right to walk along the path to the left of the church building and arrive via **Lawrence Lane** in the high street. Turn right down the street and proceed across the narrow bridge over the **River Windrush**. At the road island bear right and walk up the pavement of the A361 road towards **Fulbrook**. After about 400 yards, go right by **Cotland House** and walk along the footpath that arcs left over a stile/footbridge. Continue along the backs of houses in the village of **Fulbrook** for about 400 yards and eventually bear left to arrive in **Meadow Lane**. Walk up the beautiful lane of Cotswold houses to the A361 road. Cross over the road with care, and proceed up **Church Lane** opposite. Stroll along the footpath that goes to the left of the church building and exit the churchyard via a stile, aiming for

another stile straight ahead. Here you arrive in **Upper End** and turn right to reach the A361 road once again. Go left up the side of the A361 road for 50 yards then cross over the main road, go through the kissing gate and walk the clearly signed footpath into open countryside. Initially you walk to the left of the field hedge and then bear left on a well-walked footpath over cultivated land. After passing through a couple of hedge gaps you enter woodland and **Widley Copse**. (2¹/₄ miles)

② Head to the right along the fine track among the trees and soon you will be walking in delightful open

THE WELCOMING MAYTIME INN

countryside, descending the track in a generally south-east direction. After passing **Paynes Farm**, you reach a junction of tracks and turn right up a walled track to a farm gate. Go over the stile to its left and proceed ahead, passing close to **Faws Grove** and then descending to a stile. Take the track up to a lane and then head to the right along the lane for about 350 yards. Turn left over a stone stile and into **Dean Bottom,** strolling down the beautiful valley to its end. Here you may wish to go to the right to visit the fascinating small **church of St Oswald**.

St Oswald's church is set in the deserted village of Widford, near Swinbrook. The name 'Widford' comes from Old English 'withig ford', meaning 'the ford by the willows'. It was formerly part of Wychwood Forest, which was cleared there in about 1862. The parish once united with nearby Swinbrook, was part of St Oswald's Priory, Gloucester, from 1086 until the Dissolution. It was sold to the Harman family, and later to Sir Edmund Fettiplace, in 1680.

The church is all that remains of the old village, which in the 14th century consisted of thirteen houses close to the church, a mill, a manor house and farm buildings. Now standing alone in a hilly field near the River Windrush, the 12th-century

St Oswald's church is a sad and lonely sight. It was built over the remains of a Roman villa and some Roman paving can still be seen in the chancel. The delightful small church has been used as a film set, including that for the marriage of Lorna Doone in the TV series.

Back on the path, head left to take the riverside footpath into the village of **Swinbrook**, where a narrow walled path leads to **St Mary's church** (a visit inside is worthwhile). Note the fine wool merchants' graves in the churchyard then exit onto the road. (1³/₄ miles)

③ Turn right and continue down the road past the lovely Cotswold buildings and, at the corner, near the **Swan Inn**, go left over a stile to walk the signed footpath below the trees of **Chalk Hill Cover**. Proceed along the side of the **River Windrush** until you arrive at a stile onto the road near to a road bridge. Turn right and follow the road into **Asthall** village to visit the **Maytime Inn**.

The traceable records show that ancient Asthall was given first by William the Conqueror to Roger d'Ivery, and later by Henry III to Richard, Earl of Cornwall.

The beautiful parish church of St Nicholas dates mainly from the 12th century and sports a fascinating tower clock dating from about 1665. It was probably made by a local blacksmith; unfortunately, it is an inaccurate timepiece.

At the back of the church you will see a 17th-century manor house. This fine Jacobean building was bought by John Mitford, the 1st Baron Redesdale, Lord Chancellor of Ireland in 1806, and the Mitford family were involved for a number of years. Now it is privately owned.

Take time to visit the fine church at the end of the road and then continue to the road junction. Go left along the roadside for about 150 yards to the next road junction. (2 miles)

④ Here, turn right up a signed track into the lovely countryside. The track is initially to the left of the field hedge and then changes to the right when you reach an opening – you will see **Flat Barn Farm** to the right. The track leads up to the busy A40 road; cross with great care and continue along the signed footpath opposite, walking to the left of the field hedge. After about 350 yards, turn right through the hedge and follow the direction of the fingerpost through a series of tall kissing gates. As you pass through some of the enclosures on **Sturt Farm and Stud** you may see deer to the right. After passing to the left of the farm/stud

you reach a fence and exit onto a farm track. Turn right along the track back to the A40 road. Cross the road with care, and continue ahead through a farm gate onto a lovely green farm track going generally northwards. The track takes you through several farm gates and you will enjoy the fine view ahead over the **Windrush Valley**. You will see Dean Bottom and soon St Oswald's church will come into view – lovely walking indeed. All too soon you will arrive at the road in the hamlet of **Widford**, with the old mill (now a private residence called **Mill Race House**) opposite. (2³/₄ miles)

⑤ Head to the left along the road and at the first bend bear right over a stile into farm fields and walk by the side of the lovely **River Windrush**. Walk along the clear, well-used footpath, which continues near to the river, going over a series of stiles until you reach the road once again – this is **Tannery Lane**. Head to the right along the pavement of the lane for just over ¹/₂ mile into the town of **Burford,** and then turn right down the road called **Guildenford**, bearing right at its bottom to return to the car park. (1³/₄ miles)

Date walk completed:

CASSINGTON
AND THE
OXFORD CANAL

OXFORD CANAL LEVER BRIDGE

Distance:
7¹/₂ miles

Map: OS Explorer 180 – Oxford, Witney & Woodstock

Starting point:
Oxford Canal bridge number 228, Sandy Lane, Kidlington. GR 489133

How to get there: *Kidlington is 6¹/₂ miles north of Oxford. Leave Oxford on the A4144, bearing right onto the A4165 to pass through Summertown and proceed onto the A4260 (Banbury road) into Kidlington. In the town, go left up Yarnton Road then bear right onto Sandy Lane. The small car park is on the left just before you reach the Oxford Canal bridge.*

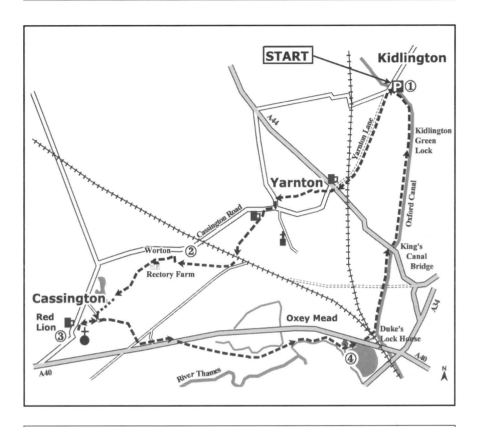

*T*his easy walk starts by the Oxford Canal and takes you along the side of a straight 'white' road into the village of Yarnton. Following the construction of new residential estates in the village some of the original footpaths (certainly many appearing on Explorer map 180) have been altered and it is interesting to experience the changes in the area – it is an adventure in itself to follow the route through the village. There is very pleasant Oxfordshire countryside to enjoy on the way from Yarnton to Cassington, where you are guaranteed a warm welcome at the Red Lion pub. The return journey brings you near to the River Thames (or Isis) and then joins the Oxford Canal near Wolvercote. Finally, you can enjoy an easy stroll along the towpath of the Oxford Canal and watch the boating world go by.

The Red Lion is a popular meeting place for locals but at this 16th century village pub everyone is made to feel welcome. During the week the real ales of London Pride, Greene King and Tetley's can be supped from 12 noon to 2.30 pm and in the evening from 7 pm to 11 pm. Saturday lunchtime opening is between 12 noon and 3.30 pm. Sunday lunchtime opening is between 12 noon and 3 pm and evening opening from 7 pm to 10.30 pm.

Good pub food is the order of the day and between the hours of 12 noon and 2 pm you may select from the appetising menu – perhaps spicy potato wedges with melted cheese, a jacket potato filled with delicious tuna or maybe a toasted sandwich. There is a lovely large garden to enjoy the summer weather to the full and, if you like to start your walking day on a full stomach, why not call in for the 'Full Monty' breakfast.

| **Telephone:** *01865 881371; e-mail: red-lion@fsnet.co.uk*

The Walk

① From the small car park in **Sandy Lane**, **Kidlington** cross over bridge **number 228** of the **Oxford Canal** and proceed along the lane. After about 25 yards the lane bends right and here you bear left to walk to **Yarnton Lane** on the waymarked footpath set to the left of the hedge. Proceed along this easy path going south-westwards in a fairly straight line with cultivated fields to your left. You can walk along Yarnton Lane, which runs parallel, if you prefer but it does tend to be rougher walking and there is some litter on the lane. After about 3/4 mile of easy walking, you will go onto the lane to go over a railway crossing and can then return to the hedge-side path to complete the route to the A44 road at **Yarnton**.

Fine meadows spread like a green carpet before the pleasant houses of Yarnton. By the green is a house that looks like a giant beehive but, in fact, is a round and heavily thatched house, with one room up and one room down.

The charming Jacobean manor in Yarnton, with great chimney stacks and curved gables, was built in 1612 by Sir Thomas Spencer, whose coat of arms is pierced at the corners with holes for muskets. Sir Thomas Spencer was an ancestor of the Spencer family of Althorp and he rebuilt the lofty tower of the Norman church. Yarnton has a rare 19th-century brass portrait – that of a young man with hair to his

*shoulders, in a rich, furred gown
and cloak – with this record of his
love for his village inscribed
below:*

*'Yarnton! my childhood's home!
Do thou receive
This parting gift:
My dust to thee I leave.'*

*He had already given the church
its font and its sculptured reredos
and, dying at the age of 87 in
1826, he left a name to be long
and affectionately remembered
here – William Fletcher.*

Cross over the busy A44 near to
the road island and proceed ahead
on a waymarked path that takes you
through to the **Cassington** road.
Cross over the road and enter the
residential estate opposite. Bear left
into **Great Close** and follow this
round until you see a waymarker to
The Paddocks sited by a small
bridge. Follow the waymarker
direction and you will soon be
walking along a quiet residential
road of that name. Follow this road
until you reach a T-junction at
Rutten Lane. Go left along **Rutten
Lane** to arrive back on the
Cassington road. Now head right
and then go left up a waymarked
footpath signed 'Cassington 1' and
sited at the end of a pub car park.

THE RED LION IS A POPULAR MEETING PLACE

You will enter a fairly new residential estate; bear right along its tarmac footpath to reach a stile into open countryside. Continue along the good, well-used footpath, taking the right fork and passing though trees into the next field. Again take the right fork at the footpath junction, aiming generally south-west to cross a large open area. At its end bear left and walk beneath the railway bridge. Follow the waymarker direction as the path arcs right and then straightens out to continue in a westerly direction. This is very pleasant walking along a sort of green valley. At the end of the valley you will reach a set-aside field. Cross over this field, aiming for the white marker post in the trees to the right ahead. (2¼ miles)

② Go over the footbridge into the trees, and take the path through the trees to a fence. Head right up by the fence for about 60 yards and then left along a wide farm driveway, passing between the buildings of **Rectory Farm**. After passing the farmhouse, you will cross its drive and can continue along a fenced track by a wall. In a few strides you are back in open countryside, walking a good track going in a generally south-westerly direction. There is a hedge to your left and a fence to the right. The track descends into trees and you cross over a footbridge then ascend a slope to a stone stile. (Note the

amusing notice by the side of the stile, which reads, 'NOTICE TO ALL DOGS – KEEP OWNERS UNDER CONTROL AND TO PATH'). Go over this stile and walk to the left of some trees, with lakes partially visible to the right through the trees. Soon you will arrive on **Bell Lane** in **Cassington**. Head left down the lane into the village. After about 50 yards, turn right down a waymarked, walled footpath and walk this to its end, where you will arrive by the green. **The Red Lion** pub is by the road through the village. (1 mile)

Houses with thatched roofs and dormer windows cluster by the green in Cassington and from the village you look across the River Thames to a great tree-mantled hill. When you enter the church you quickly realise that this is part of Norman England: superb doorways and windows that let the church fill with light – the handiwork of Norman craftsmen is everywhere.

③ From the pub, retrace your steps to the walled footpath by crossing over the green and going left past the old post office. When you get back to **Bell Lane,** cross over and continue ahead on a waymarked path signed 'Wolvercote 2½'. This path leads you through some trees and a pleasant stretch in the shade will bring you out onto a road (a former railway line). Cross over the road and walk up to the hedge at the end of the field opposite. Bear left and walk by the side of this hedge to footbridges over another newish road. Cross this road and continue ahead through the trees on the path that runs to the left of, and parallel with, the A40 road. After about 250 yards, bear right and exit the trees onto the road. Cross the busy A40 with great care, and descend to go over the stile opposite signed 'Wolvercote 2' to arrive in pastureland. Bear left, following the waymarker direction and cross the footbridge into a very large field. To your right is the River Thames and you follow the waymarker direction, which takes you to the right of willow trees protecting a stream. After about 1 mile of pleasant, easy walking, you will arrive at a new metal gate by a link river. The route bears left and then right to continue along the side of this pleasing river. Walk along the riverside path until you reach the **Oxey Mead Nature Reserve**. (2 miles)

④ Enter the nature reserve and enjoy the delightful walk along the side of the river. Soon the footpath arcs left and you continue by the river with a large lake visible through the trees on the far bank. After about 300 yards, pass beneath the railway bridge and bear left past canal bridge no. 232 to reach the **Oxford Canal** and **Duke's Lock House**. For the remaining 2 miles of the walk, you can stroll along the towpath of the canal. This is very pleasant during the summer months, when large numbers of colourful narrowboats make their way up the canal. As you approach **Kidlington,** you pass by a number of very attractive gardens which back onto the canal and you may be lucky enough to see swans with their cygnets on the towpath. All too soon you will arrive back at canal bridge no. 228, where your car is parked. (2¼ miles)

Date walk completed:

THE CHURCHES WALK

FLAGSTONE WALL AROUND HOUSES IN FILKINS

Distance:
10¹/₄ miles

Map: OS Outdoor Leisure 45 – The Cotswolds

Starting point:
Small car park by the bus stop near to the village hall in Alvescot.
GR 271045

How to get there: *Alvescot is 6 miles south-east of Burford. From the A40 road island at the top of Burford, head towards Witney then after 3 miles bear right and continue along the B4020, passing through Shilton. At Carterton, bear right onto the B4477 and right again onto the Alvescot road. After about ¹/₂ mile, you will arrive in the village of Alvescot.*

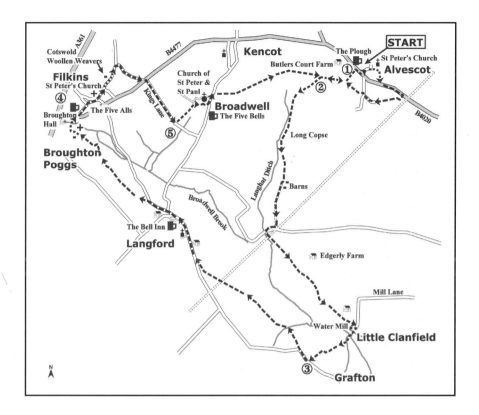

The Cotswolds' Alvescot is the starting place for an adventure in which no less than five historic churches in western Oxfordshire are visited. Initially, you pass by St Peter's church, then go over a dismantled railway line to reach a wonderful old mill at Little Clanfield; on into Langford to see the very fine church of St Matthew and then to the village of Broughton Poggs to visit its manor church. Broughton Poggs is effectively joined with Filkins near to the Five Alls, where you can rest and imbibe of the nectar before strolling past the church of St Peter. Here, unusual stone walls surround some of the cottages and you can visit the Woollen Weavers' Exhibition (sited in an 18th-century barn) before departing towards Broadwell. In this village, you can explore the church of St Peter and St Paul, which is located by a small lake in an idyllic setting.

The Five Alls, a 17th-century hostelry, is a delightful, tranquil 'olde worlde' pub, with accommodation available. Timbered ceilings, flagstone floors and crackling log fires add wonderful character. Fresh, homemade food is the order of the day – British products are used, especially meat and cheeses – and this can be selected from the menu or the specials board and eaten in the bar, by candlelight in the attractive restaurant, or perhaps in the large garden, where you can enjoy a game of giant chess on the beautifully laid out lawn chessboard.

If you are a real ale *connoisseur, the award winning Hook Norton bitter will appeal, or you may prefer Everards Tiger or one of the guest ales on offer. Telephone: 01367 860306; fax: 01367 860776; website: www.dursley-cotswolds-uk.com*

① From the car park head to the right along the main street of **Alvescot**.

Alvescot is a small village situated adjacent to RAF Brize Norton and lying between the Cotswold hills and the Thames Valley. It has a population of about 400 persons, with one pub, one shop, an excellent school, and a village hall. Like so many villages, it lost its railway under the Beeching axe and has also lost its petrol pumps and village store. The Methodist chapel has also gone. The Baptist chapel has been converted to a house, but the steps by the Shill used for total immersion baptisms can still be seen by Tanners Mill. The Plough Inn remains to quench

local thirst. 'Outwear' stands where the village store and post office once stood, and is now a thriving clothing shop.

After 15 yards, cross over the street and head up **Mill Lane** opposite, aiming towards **St Peter's church**. Walk up the lane and bear right into the churchyard, exiting via the kissing gate at the bottom and crossing pastureland to reach the B4020 road; turn left and continue along the pavement for about 300 yards. At the speed sign, turn right along a concrete driveway, past attractive residences. After 100 yards, turn right over a field stile into open countryside and follow the clear footpath towards the backs of gardens. Here, proceed ahead, bearing left then right along a lane past attractive Cotswold stone houses. In about 250 yards, head left up a lane, following the footpath sign 'Kencott 1¹/₄'. After 20 yards turn right over a field stile to walk along the clear footpath over pastureland, passing to the left of a small copse. Proceed ahead and cross the footbridge, keeping to the path up to a stone corner stile and a farm gateway. (1¹/₄ miles)

② Bear left through the gateway and diagonally cross the next field to a second gateway. Here, head right, keeping the hedge to your left. The path arcs left and soon you will be walking by the side of **Long Copse**; then pass through the farm gate by large barns onto a wide stone track. Take this track for the next ¹/₂ mile up to a hedge. Turn

right along the side of the hedge and exit onto the road via a farm gate. Cross the road and proceed over the stile opposite, walking along the **D'Arcy Dalton Way**. A narrow field leads to a second stile and the former railway line (brought into disuse by the Beeching axe). Cross this good track and head over a large cultivated field, aiming for the hedgerow set to the left ahead. Just under ¹/₂ mile further on, turn left over a footbridge and then immediately go to the right along the other side of the hedge. Initially, the path curves right and then left and you pass through several farm gates/gateways until you walk to the right of a beautiful farm cottage to

THE FIVE ALLS AT FILKINS

reach **Mill Lane** on the edge of **Little Clanfield**. Turn right along the lane, passing to the left of **Little Clanfield Mill**. Proceed along the footpath by the stream, crossing over a footbridge and a stile to arrive back in open countryside. Follow the waymarker direction and cross a second footbridge and a large field, aiming for trees at its top. Proceed through the gap in the hedge set to the right side of the trees and bear right and then left to maintain your direction. After passing some large willow trees, you will arrive on a lane. (3^1/$_4$ miles)

③ Turn right and continue on the lane for about 250 yards. Where the lane bends sharp left, proceed ahead following the footpath sign 'Langford 1' (now going north-west). After crossing a footbridge the path bears left through a hedge gap and you aim towards the tower of **Langford church** on the horizon ahead. After about 450 yards, cross over a footbridge (SP 258018) and a further cultivated field, then cross the disused railway line once again. Take the clear farm track set to the left of the hedge, maintaining your general north-westerly direction. Where the track bends left continue ahead, towards a stile on the edge of the village of **Langford**. Go over this and the next stile then bear left onto the road, arriving opposite **Hooks Close**. Head to the right up the roadside, passing the lovely

Cotswold stone cottages and houses and the impressive **church of St Matthew**, into **Langford**. Continue up the main street, passing the **Bell Inn** and bearing left along **Filkins Road**. After passing the last house on the left, walk a further ^{1}/$_4$ mile and then turn left through a farm gate and take the distinct footpath set to the right of the field hedge. After going through further gates you reach a field corner and continue over cultivated land to a stile by a farm gate. Walk up the next field to a gate. Head left to a final farm gate and here go to the right towards the farm gate set to the immediate right of a large barn on the edge of **Broughton Poggs**. Go through this gate and the farmyard, exiting via a further gate with the **church of St Peter** to your right. Go immediately left through a timber doorway into the grounds of **Broughton Hall** and follow the wide pathway, bearing right through the attractive grounds to arrive in the village of **Filkins**. Cross over the busy road with care, and proceed up the road opposite to find the **Five Alls** on the left. (2^1/$_4$ miles)

④ When you have refreshed yourself continue up the road past **St Peter's church**.

The original plans for a church in Filkins were produced by a designer/builder called Richard Pace. His plans were heavily

criticised by George Edmund Street, the diocesan architect, who proclaimed that he disliked the fact that there was no architect's name on the plans, the roof was too wide and poorly supported, there were no gutters, the vestry had a flat roof and the openings for the proposed bell were too small. The spaces between the pews were too small and he felt that people would be unable to kneel. The beautiful St Peter's church was eventually built to Street's design.

As you continue you will pass by the premises of the **Cotswold Woollen Weavers**. Soon after passing **Cross Tree Lane** and **Filkins Hall** you reach the end of this fascinating village. Here you turn right and walk the quiet lane into open countryside once again until you reach the B4477 road. Cross over the road and continue up **Kings Lane** opposite towards the village of **Broadwell**. (1½ miles)

⑤ After about 700 yards, turn left over a field stile and walk along the **D'Arcy Dalton Way** path by the side of the field hedge towards the **church of St Peter and St Paul**. At the end of the field, go over the stile and bear right to walk into the village, enjoying the fine view to your left. Immediately after passing the small lake, go left and proceed through the church gate. Bear right and exit via the lychgate onto the main road in **Broadwell**. Head left up the quiet road for about 200 yards. Turn right up a footpath signed 'Alvescot 1¼' to reach open countryside and go over a couple of stone stiles. The fields are a picture of golden yellow in the summer months before harvest. Follow the clear waymarkers over a footbridge then bear left past trees to enter a small copse and to reach the village hall and car park in **Alvescot**. (2 miles)

Date walk completed:

NORTHMOOR AND THE THAMES PATH

THE RIVER THAMES

Distance:
9 miles

Starting point:
Near the post office
in Stanton Harcourt.
GR 413058

Map: OS Explorer 180 – Oxford, Witney & Woodstock

How to get there: *Stanton Harcourt is 10 miles west of Oxford. Take the B4044 road out of Oxford and bear left onto the B4449 at the road island on the edge of Eynsham. In about 3 miles, bear left at a road island and follow the signs into the village of Stanton Harcourt.*

*A*n historic village, beautiful thatched cottages, a riverside walk and a meal at a fine pub add up to an enjoyable day here in the Oxfordshire countryside. Stanton Harcourt is a fascinating village to explore and the neighbouring village of Sutton offers a peaceful road lined with attractive thatched cottages for you to admire. A short stroll along the banks of the River Thames, in part on the Thames Path, leads to the village of Northmoor, where refreshments await at the Red Lion pub. From there you pass several appealing lakes and may be lucky enough to see one of the fishermen catch a large carp. The return to Stanton Harcourt takes you past more handsome thatched cottages for a fine view of the famous chapel, Pope's Tower and St Michael's church.

The Red Lion, situated in the heart of the village of Northmoor, is a pleasing mix of white-washed walls adorned with colourful flower-filled tubs and hanging baskets, steep roofs and dormer windows. Inside fine oak beams add character, making it an archetypal English country pub. Sited adjacent to the village's 14th-century church of St Denis, the pub was once part of the ecclesiastic complex.

Walkers are made particularly welcome and you can select your food from the inexpensive bar menu or you may prefer to eat à la carte in the dining area. The food is home prepared and cooked and is excellent, with a good choice. The pub specialises in steaks and fish, so perhaps call in the evening for one of Pauline's 'Steak Nights', which are a special occasion on Wednesday or Thursday. The traditional roast lunch is served on Sundays.

A good selection *of real ale is always on tap and in good weather you can enjoy your refreshments in the lovely garden.*
Telephone: 01865 300301.

 *The Walk*

① From the post office in Stanton Harcourt, head up to the bend in the road and proceed north-east up a waymarked tarmac footpath into a residential area.

Stanton Harcourt dates from the Bronze Age but the whole village has a feel of feudal England about it. It is situated in an area rich in

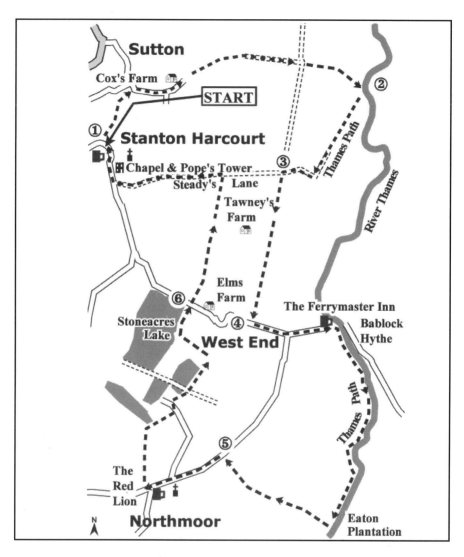

finds from the river gravels.

The village is the home of the Harcourt family, who live in the manor and are Oxfordshire's only Norman family surviving from the Conquest. The Norman church contains the tomb of Robert Harcourt, Henry Tudor's standard bearer at Bosworth Field (1485), and a visit to the chapel in the church is a must.

While the 'Harcourt' part of the

village name relates to the Norman family, 'Stanton' means 'place of the stones' in Old English. This refers to the magnificent rebuilt henge situated to the west of the village – the Devil's Quoits (a major ceremonial site in the Thames Valley 4,500 years ago). There is evidence that climatic change 200,000 years ago forced a shift in the position of the River Thames, leaving rich, fertile grasslands and large, predatory animals for early human settlers to exploit. Excavations by various agencies during the past 15 years, including the TV's 'Time Team', have revealed Stone and Bronze Age tools, burials, Beaker People's settlements and more. In excess of 900 bones and teeth of animals including mammoth, elephant, horse, bison, bear, lion and hyena have been found, many in almost perfect condition.

Once clear of the residential area, pass the infant school and then bend left past the Leys play area to walk into **Sutton**.

You can spend a pleasant time exploring the beautiful village of Sutton and it has many thatched cottages to admire. There is a history of Morris dancing in the area that principally concerns this hamlet situated to the north of the manorial estate. Until the mid 19th century the village had its own team of Morris men but today it is the Icknield Way Morris Dancers who occasionally perform here.

A CHARMING CORNER OF SUTTON

Turn right (east) and walk through the village. Pass thatched cottages and then **Cox's Farm** before going through a farm gate into the open countryside. Continue ahead as you enter pastureland and aim for the farm gate at the end of the field. Go through this gate and walk towards a stile in the far left corner of the next field. Go over this and bear right onto a good farm track set to the left of the hedge as you progress over a couple of fields. Cross over a main bridle-path and continue on a good, grass farm track. After going over a farm bridge, you soon reach a stile; go right and then left through the field hedge to progress down to the banks of the **River Thames**. (1^3/$_4$ miles)

② Turn right along the **Thames Path**. Follow the clear path that initially pulls away from the river, until you arrive on a farm track. This good track bends right and you walk along **Steady's Lane** for some 300 yards until you reach a junction of tracks. (^{3}/$_4$ mile)

③ Here, turn left to continue along the **Thames Path** as it hugs the hedge on the right-hand side and you progress over a number of farm fields. After about a mile of easy walking, go through a metal bridle-gate onto a lane, where you will see that the path you have taken leads to 'Pinkhill Lock 2^1/$_2$ m'. (1 mile)

④ Go left down the lane past the attractive mobile-home estate and soon you arrive by the **River Thames** near the **Ferrymaster Inn**, where you may wish to enjoy some liquid refreshment. Head right and walk along the bank of the **Thames** for the next mile. This is easy, attractive walking and you are likely to see a variety of boats on the river with bullrushes and other water plants producing an interesting stretch of fishing water. After about 1 mile, when opposite to **Eaton Plantation** (on the far bank of the Thames), go to the right, away from the **Thames Path** and the river, to reach a farm gate. Proceed through the gate and continue along a good farm track maintaining your north-westerly direction over several fields until you reach the road on the edge of the village of **Northmoor**. (2 miles)

The 14th-century church of St Denis and the Red Lion pub are the main places of interest in this quiet village. The church is noted for two fine 14th-century effigies of a knight and his lady. Nearby is the beautiful 16th-century Rectory Farm, which was once owned by St John's College, Oxford.

⑤ Go left along the roadside footpath into the centre of the village. You will pass the church before you reach the **Red Lion** on the corner. After imbibing at the pub continue along the road for about 100 yards. Turn right up **Baker Lane** and proceed through the farm gate at its end. Bear left along the back of the beautiful converted barn property then head right and follow the footpath set to the right of the field hedge. You will soon be crossing open ground towards a hedge, behind which there is a small lake. Go right at the hedge and continue along the path to its right until you reach a road. Turn left along the edge of the road for about 50 yards then turn right onto a path passing to the right of another small lake and then crossing over sand workings to reach a further lake. Proceed along the side of this fishing lake, where over 400 carp are being sought by fishermen (some of whom even sleep overnight in small tents!). Continue past the lake, maintaining your north-easterly direction for a further 125 yards. Now go left over a stile to walk in a north-westerly direction for some 300 yards. At the hedge, turn right along the waymarked footpath, with the **Stoneacres Lake** visible through the trees to your left. At the end of the lake, you will reach a country road. Bear right and

then turn left – **Elms Farm** will be to your right. (1³/₄ miles)

⑥ At the field end go over the footbridge onto a farm lane. Continue ahead and, where the lane bends sharp right, proceed ahead across the field to a farm gate. Cross over the next field, with **Tawney's Farm** to your right, then go over a pair of stiles onto a path that leads past a tree plantation and soon you will arrive at a hedge gap on **Steady's Lane**. Proceed through the gap in the hedge and head left along **Steady's Lane** towards the village of **Stanton Harcourt**. The lane leads past a small area of woodland where there are young horse chestnut trees on the right and more mature elder trees on the left. Pass by a farm gate and then a number of residential properties, some of which are delightful thatched cottages, before arriving at the main street in **Stanton Harcourt**. Head to the right up the high street and stroll into the centre of the village, taking time to visit the chapel, Pope's Tower and St Michael's church on the way back to your parked car. (1³/₄ miles)

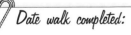 Date walk completed:

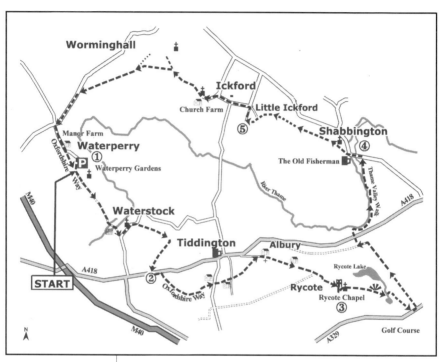

Walk 13

WATERPERRY WANDER

Distance:
11 miles

Starting point:
The car park at
Waterperry
Gardens.
GR 629084

Map: OS Explorer 180 – Oxford, Witney & Woodstock

How to get there: *Waterperry is 7¹/₂ miles west of
Thame. Leave Thame on the A418 road. After about
2 miles bear right onto the Ickford road and continue into
Worminghall. Here, go left then right onto Waterperry
Road. Waterperry Gardens are at the very end of the
village.*

BULLS LANE, ICKFORD

*T*his outing provides you with the opportunity to walk part of the Oxfordshire Way – an easy 65-mile (104 km) lowland way devised in the early 1970s to link the Cotswolds with the River Thames. It stretches from Bourton-on-the-Water to Henley-on-Thames and on this walk you will travel on a lovely section that allows you to visit English Heritage's Rycote Chapel. The route takes you along the banks of the River Thame for refreshments at one of my favourite pubs, which is just on the other side of the county boundary.

The Old Fisherman, situated on the banks of a tributary of the River Thame, is an attractive pub set in idyllic surroundings on the edge of Oxfordshire. The building has low ceilings with timber beams, log fires and tasteful decoration with a fishing theme. Each room displays items of fishing gear and/or huge fish set in glass display cases to create a unique relaxed and peaceful atmosphere. You will enjoy your refreshment break here. A warm welcome is assured and you can sit out in the terrace/garden above the sparkling Thame, with a pint in hand – a real treat.

The chef prepares bar and à la carte food to the highest standards. The bar meals are scrumptious but if an evening dinner is your desire I suggest that you call back at the Old Fisherman after your walk. The mouth waters at the very thought of grilled goat's cheese en croute with sun-dried tomato and olive oil dressing followed by rump of lamb roasted medium rare and served with a choice of a honey and thyme or Merlot and mint sauce. Perhaps finish with raspberry and hazelnut meringue served iced. This is food at its best.

The large, comfortable bar *is open daily, every lunchtime and evening, and benefits from all-day opening at weekends. Award winning Greene King beers are available and the real ales include their IPA and Morland's Old Speckled Hen. Perhaps you will be tempted by one of the excellent wines on offer. There is also an extensive garden with children's playground attractions. Telephone: 01844 201247; website: www.theoldfisherman.com; e-mail: dick@theoldfisherman.com*

 *The Walk*

Waterperry Gardens form a quiet, secluded area that reflects a medieval history – a magical place surrounded by beautiful trees, shrubs and flowers, classical borders, modern planting, secret corners and long vistas. You can visit a variety of wonderful, colourful gardens – the herbaceous border, the Mary Rose garden, the herbaceous nursery, the formal garden, the alpine garden. In spring you can enjoy a lovely river walk set with snowdrops, aconites, narcissus and primroses. The route is the haunt of moorhen and kingfisher.

① Exit the car park in Waterperry

Gardens into the main street in the village of **Waterperry**. After 20 yards go left down a footpath past houses and a farm barn to reach open land behind the garden complex. Head left along the **Oxfordshire Way** around the perimeter of the gardens – you will soon enjoy a good view of the main house. At the end of the complex bear right and maintain a south-westerly direction along a wide, hedged, stone track – this is lovely walking in the autumn when the leaves are golden. After about 1/2 mile you cross over **Bow Bridge** and pass **Waterstock Mill**.

The mill stands on a small island in the River Thame. Originally a 15th-century house with watermill, it was rebuilt in the Elizabethan period, then converted into a modern dwelling in 1957.

Walk along the mill drive to the road at the bottom of **Waterstock**.

Waterstock is a small village of medieval origin whose name comes from the Old English meaning 'water place'. St Leonard's church is the hub of the village and, being the only building large enough to house gatherings, is also used for concerts. The old rectory opposite was the home of Manoug Parikian, the celebrated violinist, who, until his death in 1987, held

a summer school for strings, and the church was filled with music during the rehearsals.

Head left up the road past the tennis court and the church. After a further 125 yards turn right, crossing a field where llamas may be at play, and continue along the route of the **Oxfordshire Way**. A couple of stiles will lead you onto a golf course to walk inside the perimeter fence until you reach a stile adorned with waymarkers. Do not go over this but head to the right, continuing along the Way, and stroll across the golf course, taking care. At the far end of the golf

THE OLD FISHERMAN SITS ON THE BANK OF THE THAME

course, exit via a stile onto the A418 road. (2 miles)

② Cross over this busy road with care, then turn left along the grass verge for about 125 yards and bear right through a kissing gate. Proceed to a metal hand-gate and go over the dismantled railway line through a metal farm gate into a large cultivated field. Aim for a stile set in the far left-hand corner, walking on the **Oxfordshire Way** to cross a couple of footbridges. The path veers left, then passes to the right of a beautiful thatched cottage on a grass track before bending left then right. Go over a field stile and continue along the Way. As you descend the slope to a gate, you will have a good view down over the village of **Tiddington**. Cross over **Albury Road** and proceed past private residences to a stile. Go over this (there is a cricket ground to your far left) and continue along the Way over fields and footbridges to arrive at a kissing gate by **Albury Grange**, and then stroll into the village of **Albury**. Proceed along the track to the left of the beautiful church and pass **Church Farm** to continue along the **Oxfordshire Way** on a wide green track. This is lovely open countryside and after almost 1/2 mile of walking you will pass to the right of **Home Farm** before entering the grounds of **Rycote Park** via a pair of stiles. (2 miles)

③ At the park drive, head right and then, at the junction of driveways, go left towards the main building. After some 50 yards, bear right to pass to the right of **Rycote Chapel** and the English Heritage admission building to enter the woodland at its rear.

The 15th-century chapel contains original furniture, two roofed pews and a superb musicians' gallery.

As you progress into the trees there is a pleasing view of the main building to your left. Follow the Way signs through the wood, keeping to the clear footpath. As you emerge from the trees, proceed ahead passing the midfield sign and noting the view over **Rycote Lake** to the left. Re-enter the woodland of **Old Paddock** and follow the footpath that leads you out to the A329 road. Here, leave the **Oxfordshire Way** by heading to the left along the grass verge of the road for just over 100 yards. Now go left over a stile onto a waymarked footpath (opposite the entrance to the **Oxfordshire Golf Club**). Walk along this clear footpath set to the right of the field hedge over three large fields until you arrive by a small copse and the dismantled railway line once again. Go left along the good track and after 130 yards turn right along the side of the trees to reach the A418 road. Cross the road with care and descend onto the path that leads by the field edge to the **River Thame**. Now take the well used footpath that meanders along the side of the river up to a road – about a mile of pleasant riverside walking (the **Thame Valley Walk**). (3¹/₂ miles)

④ Head left along the side of the road and over a couple of river bridges to reach the **Old Fisherman** pub. Proceed from the pub to bear left over a stile where the road bends right and cross pastureland (**Shabbington church** is off to your right) to a stile and a lane. Bear right and then go left over a stile into pastureland. Follow the waymarker direction over several fields towards the village of **Ickford**. The path arcs left towards a timber building. You go to the left of this and then head left past a large barn-type building, following clear footpath signs which lead you via a kissing gate into the rear of an extended private garden. The footpath emerges by the side of a private garage in **Little Ickford Close**. (1 mile)

⑤ Turn right past very attractive houses until you arrive in **Bulls Lane** near to the village pond in **Ickford**. Go left and stroll along **Sheldon Road**. At the road junction, bear right towards the **church of St Nicholas**. Enter the churchyard and exit via the stile at its rear into open pastureland – **Church Farm** is to your left. Proceed across pastureland, following the footpath signs over two fields to a footbridge. Now follow the waymark sign, going left to a corner stile. Head left across the next large field, passing by a midfield sign to a gap in the hedge. Here the path arcs left and continues over three fields to a road. Head left along the grass verge of the road to the road junction. Turn left into the village of **Waterperry**. Where the road bends left, continue ahead, following a fingerpost direction over a stile, crossing pastureland and walking along the backs of houses. At the final stile go left and return to the car park. (2¹/₂ miles)

Date walk completed:

Walk 14

DORCHESTER AND THE CLUMPS

THE SPECTACULAR VIEW FROM THE CLUMPS

Distance:
9¹/₄ miles

Starting point:
The free village car park at Bridge End, Dorchester.
GR 578941

Map: OS Explorer 170 – Abingdon, Wantage

How to get there: Dorchester is situated some 8 miles east of Abingdon. Leave Abingdon on the A415 road and at Burcot turn right onto a minor road to arrive in the village.

A walk along the bank of the River Thames, an ascent for a view of the Thames Valley and a stroll through a most beautiful medieval village – who could ask for more? On this delightful walk you can experience the beauty and history of a fascinating area of Oxfordshire. Starting from Dorchester, you walk by the side of the River Thames to the hamlet of Little Wittenham, and then ascend Round Hill for an outstanding view over the Thames, Cotswolds, Chilterns and Ridgeway. Open countryside leads to Long Wittenham, where refreshment can be taken. The walk returns along the bank of the Thames, on which a number of river craft travel, and Canada geese may keep you company. You leave the river at Day's Lock and then proceed into Dorchester to see its superb buildings.

The Vine Inn will certainly give you a warm welcome. The beautiful 16th-century, partly thatched inn, set in the peaceful village of Long Wittenham, has undergone a major redecoration. There is a superb bar menu (Old Oxford sausage, mash and gravy is something special) and lasagne, chilli, curry, steak and veggie dishes can all be finished off with one of the great puds on offer. Alternatively, you can select from the specials board and here the 11 oz fillet steak on garlic potatoes with mushroom sauce will test the strongest appetite. Good home-cooked food is the order of the day. Food is available during the week from 12 noon to 2.30 pm and from 7 pm to 10 pm (10.30 pm on Saturday), while on Sunday you can enjoy a roast lunch between 12 noon and 4 pm.

The real ales *Morland Original and IPA are on tap, together with guest beers. Children and dogs are welcome in the large garden.*
Telephone: 01865 407 832; fax: 01865 407175;
website: www.gastro-pubs.co.uk

The Walk

① From the Bridge End car park, go left past the toilet block and St Birinus' church, and then bear right down **Wittenham Lane**. At the end of the lane continue ahead on a footpath that leads down to the banks of the River Thames – you will go over pastureland, passing a stream that runs into the main river. Turn right and then follow the

DORCHESTER AND THE CLUMPS

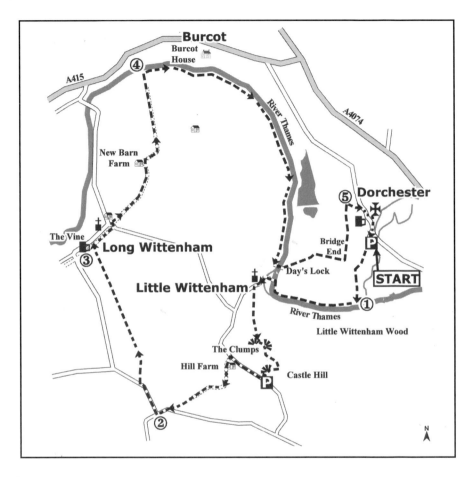

Thames Path along the banks of the **River Thames** for about ¹/₂ mile. This is lovely walking, with the river to your left, where you may see ducks, swans, coots and moorhens, and perhaps a red kite or buzzard high in the sky. Boats are likely to be on the river and as you progress around the river bend you will arrive at **Little Wittenham Bridge**. Proceed over the bridge past the Thames Conservation building onto the small island. You can walk on the island for a pleasing view over **Day's Lock**. Continue over a second bridge and stroll up the lane to see the beautiful 14th-century **church of St Peter** in **Little Wittenham**.

Little Wittenham is a tiny hamlet set at the foot of the Sinodun

Hills, better known as Wittenham
Clumps, from the top of which
there is a fine view over the
Thames Valley. The Clumps are a
favourite place for walking and
kite-flying; and they are also
historically important, Castle Hill
being the site of an Iron Age fort
and pottery. They are now part of
the Little Wittenham Nature
Reserve, which comprises an
amazing variety of woodland,
grassland and freshwater habitats
where more than 120 bird and 30
butterfly species have been seen.

From the church proceed through
the hand-gate opposite and take the
clear footpath to the top of
Wittenham Clumps to enjoy a

superb view over Dorchester and the
surrounding countryside. Continue
by going left around the **Clumps**
and then ascend the steps onto
Castle Hill and proceed into the
trees. At the path junction, turn right
and a well-used footpath will lead
you back into the open where you
arc left to reach a road by a car
park. Head to the right along the
road for about 375 yards.
Immediately after passing **Hill Farm**,
go left up a signed path and walk
past the farm buildings. Continue up
a green farm track into open
countryside. Initially the track aims
south and then bends right – lovely
walking. Walk to the left of the field
hedge and then switch to the right
as you near the road. A stile leads

HIGH STREET, DORCHESTER ON THAMES

onto the road and you head right along its edge towards **Long Wittenham**. (3¼ miles)

② At the bend in the road, bear right and then, just after the next road bend, go right over a stile and walk on the clear footpath set to the left of the field hedge. After walking this good path for about 1 mile, you will arrive in the village of **Long Wittenham** at a track. Here go right and you will find the **Vine Inn** on the left – you may enter through the rear garden. (1¼ miles)

Long Wittenham is a Thames-side village of a thousand people which sits on a quiet yet historic site. Archaeological remains ranging from a mammoth's tooth to an Iron Age shield, from a Viking-age bracelet to a Roman brooch have been found in the parish, in addition to a complete Iron Age village and a large Saxon cemetery. One of the most famous finds is a delicate, small, enamelled Roman (2nd century) tunic pin. The village cross, the base of which dates from the 7th century, by tradition marks the spot where St Birinus preached and converted the pagan Saxons to Christianity.

St Mary's church is an historic building. Walter Giffard, 3rd Earl of Buckingham, rebuilt the village church in 1120 in the Norman style, using white stone from

Caen. The end of the 13th century saw the carving of a crusader knight, the smallest effigy in England. It is believed to have been commissioned by Joan of Acre, second daughter of King Edward I.

During the Civil War, the churchwardens, fearing that Cromwell's soldiers would melt down the lead font for bullets, surrounded the font with a wooden packing case. There it remained hidden for 200 years until it was discovered and restored in 1839. The wood from the case was used to build the small table which now sits just inside the church.

③ From the **Vine Inn**, return to the track at its rear and head left. Pass along the backs of houses and soon pass the **Machine Man**, a former pub that has become bed and breakfast accommodation (a really good English breakfast is offered). At the lane junction go left and then right onto a tarmac path to pass a converted, thatched property – the windows in the roof look out of place. Soon the tarmac gives way to grass and you will be walking along a wide, hedged track in a northerly direction until you reach the **River Thames**. (1½ miles)

④ At the river, turn right along the **Thames Path**. You will pass **Burcot House** and the Chester Homes premises on the opposite bank and are likely to see grebe, herons, ducks, moorhens, coots and, of course, Canada geese – I saw a grebe with a fish in its beak. Boats (small and large) will pass you as you progress along the path, going through a series of bridle-gates before you reach **Day's Lock**. Cross over the **Thames** at **Day's Lock** and pause to watch the superb boats – it is always a pleasure to see the lovely craft making their way through a fine lock gate. When you are ready exit the lock area via the hand-gate and follow the direction of the waymark post towards **Dorchester**. The path leads to a clear footpath, passing mounds, with cultivated fields to your left. In about 1/4 mile, go left along a path that leads up to the edge of bushes and houses in the village.

Dorchester is a most charming and picturesque place set amidst water meadows by the confluence of the River Thame and the River Thames. You can lose yourself in the beauty of the village, where many period buildings line the streets and there are superb thatched cottages to admire. The

wonderful abbey is one of the largest churches in Oxfordshire. It stands on the site of a Saxon cathedral built by St Birinus in the 7th century and is set in beautiful gardens. The unique Jesse window is a 'must see' feature.

Head up this path and soon you can bear right to arrive in the village on **Watling Lane**. Go left along this quiet lane for some 300 yards. You pass a number of attractive houses and a beautiful thatched cottage. (2³/₄ miles)

⑤ At **19 Watling Lane**, go right up a footpath waymarked 'High Street' and stroll through to the main street in the village. You pass a further attractive thatched cottage as you arrive in the high street. Turn right and stroll along the superb street – the post office is a particularly fine building. Go through the lychgate on your left to see the abbey. Exit the churchyard at the front and proceed through the hand-gate onto the main road. Cross over the road to return to your car. (¹/₂ mile)

Date walk completed:

THE GREAT BARN

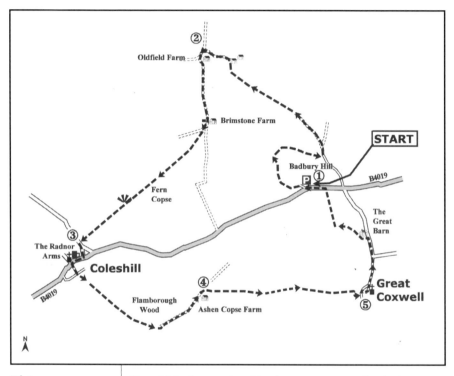

Distance:
7¼ miles

Starting point:
Badbury Clump
car park.
GR 263946

Map: OS Explorer 170 – Abingdon, Wantage & Vale of White Horse

How to get there: *Great Coxwell is about 3 miles west of Faringdon. Leave Faringdon on the B4019 road. There is an NT car park off to the right just past the Holloway Road turning into Great Coxwell.*

A fine walk through woodland to an old country estate and a visit to a famous medieval barn form part of your adventure in this lovely area on the edge of the Cotswold Hills. The circuit starts from Badbury Hill (with a beautiful bluebell wood in the spring) and takes you across rolling Oxfordshire countryside to step back in time in Coleshill – a lovely village preserved by the National Trust. After strolling through the park, you cross typical undulating countryside to reach the attractive village of Great Coxwell, where there is an old church to visit before you make your way up to see the National Trust's wonderful Great Barn. A final short uphill stretch offers fine retrospective views of the barn.

The Radnor Arms is an old stone building in an attractive setting bordering Coleshill Park. Originally the village smithy, the building was changed by local workers to a village pub in 1949, but it retains a good display of farming and smithy tools in the Smithy Bar. The pub, which is owned by the National Trust, is built on a split level and is a friendly and popular local, serving beers from casks behind the bar.

You are assured of a superb pint at the Radnor Arms, for the landlord is an advocate of quality real ale and constantly changes those offered. Normally the ales on tap are from local breweries within a 25 mile range of the pub. The Radnor Arms also has a very good reputation for its high-class food. All the meat is provided by the local butcher and the food is home-cooked on the premises.

Open every lunchtime, *this quaint pub's meals can be enjoyed indoors or in its pleasing gardens. Telephone: 01793 861575.*

The Walk

Badbury Clump is an attractive area of mainly beech trees under the care of the National Trust. Some 2,500 years ago it was the site of an Iron-Age settlement but *the exposed sandy outcrop has been eroded over time. It was largely levelled early in the 19th century, but the circular earthen rampart and ditch are still visible. Can you imagine the enclosed round huts, storage pits for grain and pens for livestock?*

THE GREAT BARN AT GREAT COXWELL

① If you are doing the walk in the spring, spare the time to stroll up the well-used path to the right of the parking area to enjoy a most superb display of bluebells in **Badbury Clump**. Otherwise, proceed over the stile into the main area of woodland and follow the clear wide footpath into the trees. After about ¹/₂ mile of pleasant walking through the trees, you will reach a junction of footpaths. Here, turn right and exit the **Clump** via a further stile. After about 150 yards, bear right to join the footpath coming in from the left. This footpath hugs the edge of the woodland as you progress in an easterly direction. You will have a view up to **Badbury Clump** to your

right and then you enter the trees and continue until you reach a lane. Head left along the lane and soon reach a farm gate. Go over the stile to the left of the gate and bear left to walk on a green track to the right of the woodland. Follow the waymark signs as the track arcs right and then left to become hedged – a lovely stretch of easy walking. At the end of the trees, bear left over a stile and now aim north-west generally towards **Oldfield Farm**. At the farm gate, go through the kissing gate and walk along the bridle-path past a row of terraced farm cottages. The path arcs left and soon you will be approaching the main farm complex. Continue along the track to the right of the farm buildings. (2 miles)

② Bear left and walk along the concrete driveway to **Brimstone Farm**. When you reach the farm, bear right and then right again, looking out for a stile set in the fence to the left. Go over this stile and cross pastureland to a pair of stiles then bear right and take the footpath set to the left of the field hedge, descending towards the trees in **Fern Copse**. A stile and a footbridge will take you through the trees and then you commence an ascent of the hill opposite, walking to the left of the field hedge. At the top of the hill there is a fine view towards **Buscot** and on a clear day you may be able to spot **Buscot House** (NT). Continue in a generally south-westerly direction until you reach the road. (1½ miles)

Situated between Lechlade and Faringdon, neo-classical Buscot House is a delight and in the saloon are several Pre-Raphaelite paintings, including the series 'The Legend of the Briar Rose', purchased in 1890. The 1st Lord Faringdon began the wonderful art collection that is one of Buscot's main attractions today, and in 1962 the house, set in lovely grounds that slope down to

THE RADNOR ARMS WAS ONCE THE VILLAGE SMITHY

a lake and a water garden, passed into the care of the National Trust.

③ Turn left then cross the road and go down the lane to the right into **Coleshill** – the **Radnor Arms** is just round the corner to the right.

Coleshill is a pretty village built of Cotswold stone on a steep hill leading down to the River Cole and the Wiltshire border. In the 18th century the Pleydell-Bouverie family (the Radnor Earls) owned the village and it was then part of the Coleshill Estate – the family lived in Coleshill House. Sadly, the splendid 17th century mansion was burnt down in 1952 during building renovations. Nevertheless, substantial outbuildings remain and the estate and pub are now administered by the National Trust. Coleshill House left its mark in nearby Faringdon, as its classical style was imitated in the houses built by wealthy 18th-century merchants when the town began to prosper.

Proceed down the main street in **Coleshill**, passing the village green and the **church of St Faith and All Saints**, where you will find a memorial to Sir Mark Pleydell. Continue by walking down the lovely lane opposite **Church Lane** and after a few yards go over a stile into beautiful **Coleshill Park**. Follow the clear waymark signs and descend through the parkland in a south-westerly direction, going over a few stiles; soon you will be ascending towards the right-hand corner of **Flamborough Wood**. Pass by a clump of trees and then curve left to walk a good green track that leads you to the right of the trees and to **Ashen Copse Farm**. (1^1/$_2$ miles)

④ Pass to the left of the farm complex and the large barns then bear right and go over a field stile, aiming for a further stile in the field's bottom left corner. You are now walking in an easterly direction and should proceed over several fields, going over stiles and passing through kissing gates, towards the village of **Great Coxwell** ahead. As you approach the village, walk to the right of the field hedge and then arc right. Then go left to enter **Great Coxwell** via a hedged footpath and to arrive in **Holloway Road**. (1 mile)

⑤ Head left along the road into the village and enjoy the pleasing view up the main street.

The little village of Great Coxwell is very old – a quiet place of stone cottages, colourful gardens and narrow lanes. In the early 13th century, the entire village, including its parish church, was owned by the Cistercian abbey which King John had founded in 1204 at Beaulieu in Hampshire. The small village hall and attractive church are at one end of the village, along with some more modern housing, while the celebrated Great Barn is located at the other. The Norman parish church of St Giles stands in its award-winning churchyard on a ridge above the village and is one of the landmarks of the Vale of the White Horse.

To visit the church, bear right up the footpath and the **church of St Giles** is to the right. Pause here to admire the churchyard and to enjoy the view over the surrounding countryside. From the churchyard, proceed ahead along the lane to arrive back on **Holloway Road**. Stroll up the road until you reach the **Great Barn,** set back to the left.

The massive Great Barn was built of Cotswold stone in the 13th century as a cell of the Cistercian abbey of Beaulieu. It measures *152 ft long by 44 ft wide and is 48 ft up to the ridge. After the dissolution of the monasteries in the 16th century, the Great Barn passed to the Mores family. In the 18th century it went to the Pleydell-Bouveries and became part of the Coleshill Estate. A Mr E. E. Cook purchased the building in 1945 and he bequeathed it to the National Trust in 1956.*

Exit the grounds of the **Great Barn** via the gateway at the back of the building and bear right to walk along the field edge towards woodland. The path circles the edge of the field and you enter the trees over a stile. A final stile takes you back out of the woodland and you bear right to ascend to the edge of the trees. Soon you will be in open countryside and ahead of you will be the **B4019** road. At the road bear left and walk along its grass verge back to **Badbury Clump** car park. (1¼ miles)

Date walk completed:

EWELME
TREASURE

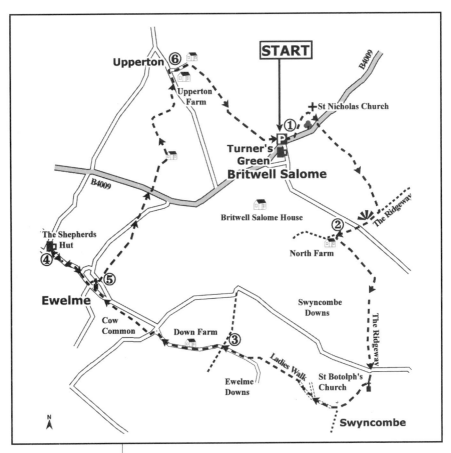

Distance:
10 miles

Map: OS Explorer 171 – Chiltern Hills West

Starting point:
The small layby by
the telephone box
in Britwell Salome.
GR 671932

How to get there: Britwell Salome is 15½ miles south-
east of Oxford. Leave Oxford on the A4074 (Reading road).
After about 11 miles turn left onto the B4009 Watlington
road and, in a further 3 miles, follow the signs into Britwell
Salome.

FIELD PATH BETWEEN UPPERTON AND BRITWELL SALOME

A hike along part of the Ridgeway is always a pleasure and this splendid walk takes you onto a particularly fine stretch of this famous path. From Britwell Salome, the route passes St Nicholas' church, crossing the main road onto a superb farm track that leads to the Ridgeway. Open views can be enjoyed as you walk along the way, with the scenery around Swyncombe Downs a special treat. You can visit the old church of St Botolph and then stroll along lovely tracks and paths past Down Farm. The pastureland ascent into Ewelme is a delight and you are greeted by the sight of a most beautiful village where time seems to stand still. After you have refreshed yourself at the Shepherds Hut, the route takes you across open countryside and through the small village of Upperton before crossing cultivated fields to arrive back in Britwell Salome.

The Shepherds Hut was built in 1870 for drovers taking sheep from Thame to Reading. It is set in the village near to a watercress river and offers a warm welcome to all walkers. Traditional, rustic-style decor, exposed beams, part exposed wooden floors and a general feeling of ease create a friendly atmosphere in which to enjoy a refreshment break. You can mix with locals, trade stories and swap gossip in the bar while partaking from the great selection of beers, wines and spirits. Ruddles Best and Morland Original are the two real ales on tap.

The pub specialises in good English cooking. Bangers and mash with onion gravy is a smash hit with locals, and the sticky toffee pudding is probably the best you will ever eat.

On a warm summer day, the enclosed garden is a special treat, providing a safe, secure place for the young to explore, and a quiet spot to enjoy a drink. Telephone: 01491 825661; e-mail:Cambell.White@virgin.net

The Walk

① From the lay-by, proceed north-eastward up the side of the B4009 road for 125 yards, then go left through a hand-gate onto a public footpath and walk to the left of the field hedge to a lane. Here, head left along the lane to visit the **church of St Nicholas**.

For centuries there were two parishes, Britwell Salome and Britwell Prior. The former was in the diocese of Oxford but the latter was attached to the priory and convent of Canterbury. In 1154 Henry II destroyed the castle at Britwell on his way to relieve Wallingford Castle, and all that remains of Britwell Castle is a wooded mound on the hill and a deep ditch that could have been part of the moat. An arrow's flight from what used to be the priory chapel stands the 13th-century church of St Nicholas. The age of the ancient yew tree in the churchyard is declared in a certificate in the church porch, and would have been a hundred years old when young Alfred was battling with the invading Danes – perhaps it supplied the bowmen at Agincourt with some of their trusty longbows. Its enormous girth has housed very many generations of foxes in the earths at its base.*

Proceed through the signed hand-gate opposite the church entrance and take the footpath that leads back to the B4009 via a stile. Head right then go left and cross the B4009 onto a good farm track going generally south-east. Walk along this hedged track for almost 1/2 mile, until you reach a junction of tracks and the **Ridgeway**. Turn right along the **Ridgeway** and enjoy the good view to your right that embraces **Britwell Salome House** on the hill. Cross over a lane and in a further 300 yards arrive near to **North Farm**. (2 miles)

② Head left past the farm and go up the hedged footpath towards **Dean Wood** – fine walking. As you ascend, follow the **Ridgeway** waymarkers through beautiful open countryside, arcing to the right into the trees and then following the track to the left of a field hedge up to the lane near to **Swyncombe**.

The name of Swyncombe is derived from the Old English words 'swin' (meaning wild boar) and 'cumb' (meaning flank of the hill), all of which suggests that there was a Saxon settlement here and probably wild boar were hunted in the woodlands nearby.

Cross over the lane and descend past the fascinating **St Botolph's church**.

St Botolph's is an 11th-century Crusader church and is one of only 64 in the country so named. It contains fine brasses and a rather exceptional effigy tomb. The church is set in the Chiltern Hills adjacent to the Ridgeway, on which pilgrims have walked for centuries. Snowdrop Sunday, when

THE SHEPHERDS HUT WAS ORIGINALLY BUILT FOR THE DROVERS TAKING SHEEP TO READING

the snowdrops in the churchyard are in full bloom, is an annual event held in February.

If you have time, why not visit the charming village of Swyncombe, which radiates from an attractive green. An avenue of cypress trees leads back to the church, where a glorious copper beech tree adds colour in the autumn.

Continue along the **Ridgeway** route onto a good hedged track through the trees. About 600 yards after passing by the church, the **Ridgeway** bends left into woodland. Here, continue ahead on a bridleway track known locally as **Colliers Bottom** with trees to your left and a more open view to your right. In 650 yards, Colliers Bottom bends right and you bear left onto a bridleway path called **Ladies' Walk**. The track leads you out of the trees into farm fields and for the next 500 yards you walk to the left of the field hedge. The path enters trees and you emerge on the driveway of **Ewelme Downs House**. Turn right on the driveway, going away from the house. (2¹/₂ miles)

③ After crossing the **Swans Way** track, you pass the complex of **Down Farm**. In a further 600 yards bear left to reach the road through a pair of gates. Go left along the road for 15 yards, then turn right through a kissing gate into a large

field called **Cow Common**. (Where have all the cows gone?) The delightful path crosses the field, heading towards kissing gates giving onto the road in the far top corner – you have arrived in **Ewelme**.

Ewelme is a tiny, historic village, and surprisingly off the beaten track! It has one shop-cum-post office and one pub, the Shepherds Hut, which serves delicious, very un-pub-like meals. The village is set in some of the most beautiful countryside in England, around the pool in which Anne Boleyn swam with Henry VIII, and it has a manor house which contains the swing where Elizabeth I played as a child. The old primary school is an impressive building, which was founded by Alice Chaucer, Duchess of Suffolk.

Head left along the high street through the village, passing by The Old Coach House and the old primary school. The **Shepherds Hut** pub is at the far end of the village opposite the watercress stream. (1¹/₂ miles)

④ From the **Shepherds Hut** retrace your steps back into the village and go left up **Burrows Row** to reach the wonderful church. (¹/₂ mile)

The parish church is built in Perpendicular style and the chapel of St George is particularly interesting for its inside walls are covered in medieval black letter calligraphy. The inscription on the tomb of Thomas Chaucer (son of the poet) in the same chapel is very fine. While inside the church complex you should visit the very beautiful Duchess's Almshouses. In the churchyard is a stone which reads, 'For we are labourers together with God' and beneath it lies the body of Jerome K. Jerome, the renowned writer.

⑤ Exit the churchyard by the main gate, bear right, and then go left up a waymarked track into the open countryside. The track becomes a footpath and you walk along the well prepared route across three cultivated fields. The path crosses over a lane and then you will arrive at **Grove Lane**. Cross the lane, going left and then in about 30 yards right to walk up the driveway towards an attractive farm complex called **Brightwell Grove**. Follow the clear, signed footpath that takes you to the left of the farm complex and continue to the right of the field hedge over two fields until you reach a wire fence. Here, turn right along the side of the fence and follow the waymarkers that direct you left and then right until you arrive on the road in the village of **Upperton**. Head left along the side of this quiet road for about 200 yards. (2 miles)

⑥ Turn right and walk along the road past **Upperton Farm** into the main area of the village. As you progress, you pass a number of attractive houses. At the end of the row of cottages, bear right and walk along a clear, signed footpath set to the right of **Ivy Cottage**. Follow this good, well-used footpath over cultivated fields. After $1/2$ mile or so of pleasant walking you will see **Britwell Salome** in the valley ahead. Descend into the village, going over a couple of stiles as you approach, and enter a housing estate via a hedge path – there was a red kite gliding over this as I approached the village. Walk on the pavement to the main road and you will emerge opposite the **Goose Inn**. The lay-by near the public telephone is to the left. ($1\frac{1}{2}$ miles)

Date walk completed:

THE WHITE HORSE AND WAYLAND'S SMITHY

THE DELIGHTFUL WHITE HORSE INN

Distance:
9 miles

Starting point:
The National Trust
car park.
GR 294867

Map: OS Explorer 170 – Abingdon, Wantage & Vale of White Horse

How to get there: *Woolstone is 8 miles south of
Faringdon. Leave Faringdon on the A417 (Wantage road).
After about 2 miles, turn right down the B4508 towards
Fernham. Turn left just before entering Fernham and follow
the signs towards Uffington. Just before entering Uffington,
bear right and follow the signs to Woolstone. Proceed
through the village and cross the B4507 road to go up to
the NT car park.*

*T*his is a lovely walk in Ridgeway territory to visit the White Horse hill figure and Wayland's Smithy. Don't forget your camera when you take the path up to the famous Uffington White Horse, for there are many photo opportunities. At the beginning of the walk, you will stroll by the amazing horse figure and can wander around the lovely hill to see the Manger, Dragon Hill and Uffington Castle. The route takes you onto the famous Ridgeway National Trail and along beautiful tracks to reach historic Wayland's Smithy. You then descend into the village of Woolstone for refreshment before making your way back to the car park.

The White Horse Inn, situated in the peaceful village of Woolstone, was built around 1540 and is full of interest and character – a 'chocolate-box' building. Near to it is a strange, brick construction which looks like a small tower brewery standing high amongst the older buildings in the village. This was built in 1877 by a former landlord of the pub as a grudge-revenge against the occupant of Woolstone Park – the landlord began building the tall edifice as a place from which he could spy. Because the dispute was settled, the building was never completed but this strange relic of a forgotten feud remains as an addition to one of the village's old, clunch-built cottages.

By the time you reach the inn you will be ready for one of its cask range of beers – Arkell's and Hook Norton are the real ales on offer, along with guest ales, while Scumpy Jack and Blackthorn Dry will please the cider drinkers. A full bar menu as well as an à la carte menu offers a wide selection of truly appetising food and it is a delight to eat out in the attractive garden on a sunny day.

From Monday to Saturday, the freehouse is open from 11 am to 3 pm, and 6 pm to 11 pm, with food being served up to 10.30 pm. On Sunday, the opening times are 12 noon to 3 pm and 7 pm to 10.30 pm, with food available throughout those hours.
You can be assured of a warm welcome, and accommodation is available if you wish to stay in the area to complete more of the local walks. Children are allowed in the inn but dogs are not permitted.
Telephone: 01367 820726.

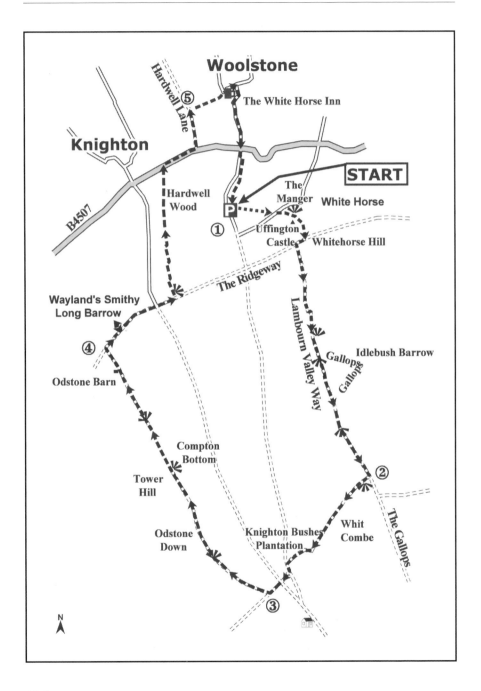

 *The Walk*

① Exit the NT car park onto the hillside and take the clear footpath towards **Whitehorse Hill**. A hand-gate allows you to cross the road and you then ascend to the top of the hill. To your left is the famous white horse.

The White Horse is an impressive sight on the chalky upper slopes of Uffington Castle, near to the Ridgeway. Measuring 360 ft by 126 ft, it is believed to be Britain's oldest hill figure – some 2,000 to 3,000 years old. There are numerous theories as to its origin, but historians believe it is Iron Age or Anglo-Saxon. The monument became very overgrown in the 19th century but it has been restored by cutting a trench to shape and infilling with chalk blocks. It is now cared for by the National Trust.
There are several nearby features to observe. The Manger is a spectacular dry valley with ripples (Giant Steps) formed by the effect of ice melting at the end of the last Ice Age. The strange flat hilltop below the White Horse is Dragon Hill and this is where legend says that St George slew the dragon – the dragon's blood was so poisonous

that the grass never grew again, hence the bare, white patches you see today. Uffington Castle is a hilltop Iron Age fort and from its crest (857 ft/262 m) you can enjoy a magnificent view over the vale that stretches as far as the Cotswolds.

Proceed past the trig point (259 m), then leave the NT area via a kissing gate to arrive on the **Ridgeway**. Go to the right along this famous walking route for just 300 yards, then head left down a clear, wide track set to the left of the fence. This lovely path zig-zags left and then right for you to continue along a good fenced path – the **Lambourn Valley Way**. The path ascends to pass to the left of some trees and then you will arrive in wide open countryside. Follow the signed route, walking between some white posts as you proceed southwards. You are walking on part of the gallops and should look out for horses being exercised. Soon, to your left, you will see **Idlebush Barrow**.

Idlebush Barrow is little more than a tiny hillock, shaped a bit like a little flying saucer sitting on the grassy plain. The small mound is about 20 ft across only and about 5 ft high.

Continue down the wide, green track and enjoy the superb views all

107

THE WHITE HORSE AND WAYLAND'S SMITHY

around. To your left is **Kingston Warren Down** and you can enjoy this lovely easy walking for a further $1/2$ mile to reach a junction of tracks. (2 miles)

② Go right and continue the gentle descent along a wide bridleway set to the left of the fence – ahead of you is a lovely valley view as you go down towards the trees of **Knighton Bushes Plantation**. The track curves right and then passes to the side of the plantation. At the top, bear left and then right to continue in a south-westerly direction. You will pass by a junction of tracks near to a small plantation of shrubs and trees and then gently ascend for the next 200 yards. ($1^{1}/_{2}$ miles)

③ Head to the right up a bridle-path, now walking in a generally north-westerly direction. The path forms a division between large cultivated fields as you progress up the edge of Odstone Down into Compton Bottom. A couple of footpaths cross your route and after about $1^{1}/_{2}$ miles of pleasant, easy ascent you will arrive at a line of trees. Proceed around the felled tree set to prevent vehicles from being driven across the cultivated land and continue north-west on a good farm track. After a further 100 yards, you will arrive at a junction of tracks. (2 miles)

④ Head to the right along the **Ridgeway**. After 250 yards bear left to visit **Wayland's Smithy**.

Wayland's Smithy is a prehistoric site given its name by Saxon settlers, for they imagined that it was the work of one of their gods, Wayland the smith. A legend grew that Wayland would re-shoe any traveller's horse left, along with a silver penny, beside the tomb. However, it is thought that the 'invisible' smith may have been linked to this site for many centuries before the Saxons recognised him as Wayland. Ancient Britons may have offered money here to a local god.

The famous smithy comprises a neolithic long burial chamber measuring 185 ft long and 43 ft wide at the south end, and is situated in a sheltering grove of beautiful beech trees. A series of gigantic sarsen stones, the tallest standing 10 ft high, are arranged in a line at the entrance at the south end and from this entrance there extends a passage 20 ft long with an opposing pair of chambers and a terminal chamber. Built between 3700 and 3400 BC, it is at least 1,000 years older than Stonehenge. It was constructed in two periods. The first construction was a ridged wooden mortuary hut with a stone floor, where fourteen bodies were found, surrounded by sarsen boulders and heaped over with chalk. The mortuary hut disappeared with the construction of the present arrangement of chambers.

Return to the **Ridgeway** and continue north-east along the good, hedged track. Just 200 yards after crossing over a track junction, go left and leave the **Ridgeway** by walking across the cultivated field along a footpath – up to your right you will see **Uffington Castle**. After about 500 yards of easy, pleasant walking, the footpath continues along a hedged stretch where you will get some shelter on a hot sunny day. The path proceeds down the left edge of **Hardwell Wood** and soon you will arrive at the B4507 road. Head to the right along the grass verge for about 300 yards then go left and stroll down a hedge track called **Hardwell Lane**. (2 miles)

⑤ After walking along the pleasant track for about 450 yards, leave it by turning right over a field stile and proceed along the edge of two fields to arrive at a stile by a farm gate. Stroll along the lane, going

CROP CIRCLES NEAR THE WHITE HORSE

ON THE ROUTE NEAR UFFINGTON CASTLE

eastwards past some attractive houses, and soon you will arrive at the **White Horse Inn**. Proceed past the inn and head right at the road junction to walk through the village of **Woolstone**.

Continue up the lane in the village as it bends right and then left and soon you cross over the **B4507** road

to take the lane up to the NT car park. After about 50 yards, bear left and go though the hand-gate onto the bottom of **Whitehorse Hill**. Head right and ascend the permissive path by the field hedge. A final hand-gate will lead you back into the car park. (1$\frac{1}{2}$ miles)

Date walk completed:

Walk 18

LETCOMBE BASSETT AND THE DOWNS

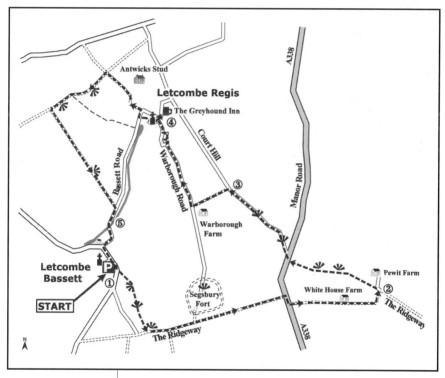

Distance:
7¹/₂ miles

Map: OS Explorer 170 – Abingdon, Wantage & Vale of White Horse

Starting point:
The church in
Letcombe Bassett.
GR 374849

How to get there: Letcombe Bassett is just 4¹/₂ miles
south-west of Wantage. Take the B4507 road from
Wantage. After 2¹/₂ miles, turn left onto the B4001 road
and follow the signs into Letcombe Bassett.

LETCOMBE BASSETT AND THE DOWNS

LETCOMBE REGIS

*T*ake your camera is my advice, for there are fine views and a number of attractive buildings to capture on film during this super walk. From the church in the pretty village of Letcombe Bassett you ascend to the Ridgeway and follow the stretch of the famous national path past Segsbury Camp. There are fine views over Castle Hill looking towards Letcombe Regis and then lanes and farm roadways lead you into the village, where refreshment awaits. Meander around the lovely village and enjoy seeing some of the loveliest thatched cottages in Oxfordshire before adjourning to the Greyhound Inn for refreshment. The route continues up a good track, passing near to Antwick's Stud to reach a lovely path set above the valley. There are super views all the way down to Letcombe Bassett and the watercress beds. A short walk down a lane takes you back up to the church.

The Greyhound Inn was built in the 17th century and is an impressive Grade II listed building. It was on the doorstep of this very inn that the Riot Act was supposedly read for the last time in England. This pub is noted for its early 19th-century brickwork which uses a Flemish bond with black glazed headers. Bearing in mind the fact that the village is very famous in the racing world as the training base of no fewer than three Grand National winners, Greyhound Inn seems a strange name

On Monday to Thursday, the pub is open from noon to 2.30 pm and from 5.30 pm to 11 pm. It is open all day from Friday to Sunday. This is a cosy place where you can relax with a pint of real ale – Morland's Original, Greene King, and Wells Bombardier are on tap, or perhaps a Blackthorn Cider is your taste – they are all in excellent cask condition in the immaculate bar.

> **Food is available** *from noon to 2 pm and from 6 pm to 9 pm throughout the week (Sunday evening food finishes at 8.30 pm). The food itself is home-cooked, hearty, wholesome and British; with soups, stews, pies and roasts flying the flag – just the measure after a morning's walk. Lunch can be enjoyed in the attractive, non-smoking, raised dining area or in the garden, if you prefer. Telephone: 01235 771093; fax: 01235 770905; e-mail: greyhound.inn@tiscali.com*

 *The Walk*

① From the church of St Michael and All Angels, head to the right up the side of the quiet road ascending **Gramps Hill**. After about 200 yards, i.e. at the first bend, bear left onto a waymarked footpath and proceed into open countryside. After about 175 yards, the path arcs right and descends into a delightful valley, then ascends rather steeply by the side of woodland. Proceed over a couple of stiles and soon you will be crossing pastureland to arrive at a final stile onto the **Ridgeway**. Turn left along the Ridgeway. You will pass by **Segsbury Fort** and can stroll up to this for a superb view over the surrounding countryside.

Segsbury Fort, sometimes called Letcombe Castle and also known as Segsbury Camp, is an Iron Age hill-fort that, together with the adjoining chalk escarpment, offers fine views over the Vale of the White Horse. A well-preserved 'vallum and fossa' (Roman defensive embankment and moat) is nearby – it is said to be more ancient than the famous White Horse of Uffington.

Continue up the wide track of the **Ridgeway** and in about ³/₄ mile you will arrive at the **A338** (**Manor Road**). Here go right for about 100 yards, then cross over the road and continue along the **Ridgeway** going generally eastwards. Shortly after passing by **White House Farm**, the track arcs left and then right. (2¹/₂ miles)

② At the right bend, go left along a hedged footpath that passes the driveway to **Pewit Farm**. This is very pleasant walking and you will enjoy some glimpses of the valley to your right through the hedge gaps. Continue along the good green track and you will arrive at the **A338** road again. Cross over the road and proceed down the lane opposite. Walk past the **Youth Hostel** and continue down **Court Hill Road**. This is easy walking and there is a fine view ahead of you over **Letcombe Regis** and **Wantage**. Proceed down the road for about ¹/₂ mile. (1¹/₄ miles)

③ Turn left along a 'white' road/ farm track that leads you past **Warborough Farm** – although the sign indicates a private road, the farmer is happy for this track to be used by walkers, but road vehicles are banned. At the end of the track, go right and head into the village of **Letcombe Regis** along **Warborough Road**. As you reach the road bend there is a cottage ahead of you

named **The Sparrow**. Until recent times this was one of two pubs in the village. Pass to the right of **The Sparrow** and then bear left by **The Anvil** (a beautiful thatched cottage) onto a hedged footpath that will lead you to the main road in the village. Head to the right, to the road junction, and then turn right up **Main Street**. The road bends left by some more thatched cottages and soon you will see the **Greyhound Inn** on your right. (1 mile)

Letcombe Regis is an historic village with three manors. The 11th-century Old Manor existed at the time of Edward the Confessor, and King John used it as a hunting lodge in the 12th century. Antwicks Manor is a 19th-century house, and Letcombe Manor, now used by the Agricultural Research Council, is late Georgian in style, set in lovely grounds with two lakes and wooded slopes by the brook.

Letcombe Regis has many architectural styles. There's the Old Vicarage (Victorian), Georgian and neo-Georgian houses and some well placed timber and thatch cottages which blend in perfectly with the rest of the dwellings throughout the winding main street.

The village has always maintained a racing tradition and you will see a number of training establishments and stableyards as you walk.

④ Retrace your steps down **Main Street** and cross over the road junction to walk past the village church. The thatched building ahead of you is stunning. Proceed past the church and then bear left along a hedged footpath that leads you to **Bassett Road**. Go to the right along the road to its corner, then head left to reach open ground. You walk up a good, well-used hedged bridle-path ascending out of the valley. To your right you can see the buildings of **Antwick's Stud** but you continue

up the hill until you reach a junction of tracks. At the track junction, head left along a green road. This is fine walking along a good track with views over **Letcombe Regis** and the surrounding countryside. After following the track for about 1/2 mile, go left and descend a clear footpath by the field hedge for about 3/4 mile to reach the **Bassett** road once again. (2 miles)

⑤ Head right along the road and soon cross a delightful bridge over a stream, where watercress once grew. You are likely to see families playing in and around the water and horses

THE HANDSOME GREYHOUND INN

come here to cool off. Continue up the road, bearing right to walk through **Letcombe Bassett**.

Letcombe Bassett is a most beautiful village. The small, friendly 12th-century church of St Michael and All Saints stands high near to Gramps Hill. It has a very modest appearance, but is a real gem and most definitely worth a visit. Look out for the scratch dials on the south buttress – these were invented by the Normans and were used to show the hour for Mass. The bells are of interest as the treble and second bells were made in 1576 in Reading by William Knight II – the only known examples by him.

Near the village's famous watercress beds, there is a thatched cottage by the brook where you are likely to see racehorses drinking. This is the source of the fictitious Arabella's Cottage in the equally fictitious Cresscombe in Thomas Hardy's novel Jude the Obscure. *The novelist Dean Swift is thought to have written some of his vitriolic political pieces whilst sitting under the ancient mulberry tree in the garden of the Old Rectory – a fine Queen Anne house.*

There used to be a pub in the village called the Yew Tree, and attached to this was the smithy – it became a private residence at the turn of the century, so the nearest pub is now in Letcombe Regis.

You pass some superb timber buildings and the **Yew Tree**. As you progress up **Gramps Hill**, you will see the church is set back to the right. (³/₄ mile)

Date walk completed:

MAPLEDURHAM DELIGHT

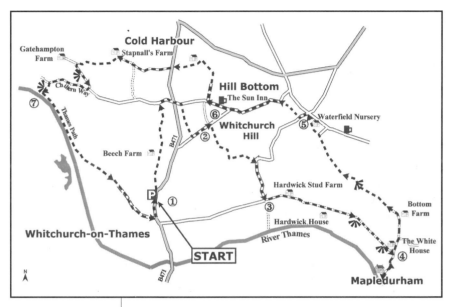

Distance:
12 miles

Starting point:
The war memorial
north of
Whitchurch-on-
Thames.
GR 633778

Map: OS Explorer 171 – Chiltern Hills West

How to get there: *Whitchurch-on-Thames is 12¹/₂ miles south-east of Didcot. Take the B4016 going south out of Didcot for 3 miles then go left onto the A417 road for 5 miles. Turn right onto the A329 at Streatley, then turn left in Pangbourne then left again onto the B471, crossing the River Thames to arrive in Whitchurch-on-Thames. Continue up the B471 for about ³/₄ mile to the war memorial.*

*T*his walk is a delight. From Whitchurch-on-Thames, you cross undulating open countryside onto Whitchurch Hill before dropping down to the estate road leading towards Mapledurham, passing Hardwick Stud Farm and the superb Hardwick House on the way. There follows a fine hill ascent during which you may be lucky enough to see red kites circling high above the trees. The woodland is a special treat in the spring with colourful wild flowers everywhere. The route passes a thatched cottage on the way to Goring Heath before reaching Hill Bottom, where you can rest for refreshments. More lovely woodland paths and part of the Chiltern Way lead to a fine view over the River Thames and the Thames Path on the way back to the war memorial.

The Sun Inn's landlord proudly boasts fine ales, good food and a hearty welcome, and I can confirm that this is the case. The Sun is very much a family inn where children and dogs under strict control are allowed. A good range of real ales is available including Brakspear and Hooray Henry, along with Strongbow cider. It is a pleasure to sit out in the garden on a sunny day in the summer and sup a pint. The inn is open every day of the week and the Sunday roast is a real plateful which will test any hungry walker.

Reasonably priced good food *is available between noon and 3 pm during the day and from 7 pm to 9 pm in the evenings. Can you say no to the Woodland Fruit Strudel?*
Telephone: 0118 9842260.

① From the war memorial, head up the road for about 100 yards, then bear left to a kissing gate into farm fields. Take the path set to the right of the field hedge over two fields, then pass through a kissing gate and continue past **Beech Farm**, following the waymarked route through hand-gates and into trees. Bear right through the next hand-gate onto a fenced footpath, going towards the gamekeeper's cottage and reach a wide track that leads to a lane. Go to the right for 160 yards to the B471 road. Cross over the road, walking towards **Hill**

THE WATERMILL IN MAPLEDURHAM

Bottom, but after 100 yards turn right down a footpath signed 'Whitchurch Hill ½'. This fairly narrow, hedged footpath leads past houses to an attractive pond as it curves left into **Orchard Combe**. Proceed down **Orchard Combe**, taking time to admire the lovely houses. At the end of the combe you reach a road almost opposite **Butler's Farm**. Head left along the side of the road for about 300 yards. (1½ miles)

② When opposite a road called **Bec Tithe**, turn right down a signed footpath, walking southwards. After you have walked about ¼ mile on the undulating hedged footpath, it arcs left and then right and eventually reaches a junction of paths/tracks. Here, go left and follow the footpath going generally south-east to reach a lane. Turn right and go down the lane (southwards) for about 600 yards until you reach a sharp right bend. (1¼ miles)

③ Head left along the estate lane signed 'Mapledurham 1½', passing by **Hardwick Stud Farm** and the entrance to **Hardwick House**, and then enjoy a fine view over the **River Thames** to your right until you reach **The White House** at a road junction. (1½ miles)

④ Head to the right down the road to visit the lovely village of **Mapledurham**.

Step back in time in the picturesque village of Mapledurham and visit the main house, which has been the home of the Blount family since the end of the 15th century. The original 12th-century manor house was replaced by Sir Michael Blount around 1588. Through their long association with the renowned 18th-century poet Alexander Pope, Martha and Teresa Blount became the most famous sisters of the family and, upon Pope's death, Martha inherited many of his possessions, which are displayed in the house. Filled with family portraits, relics and furniture from every generation, Mapledurham House represents an interesting mix of changing fashions and fortunes. The rich red bricks of the house give it a warm appearance and the small gable above the high window at the back of the house indicates that the house was a safe refuge for Catholics. The gardens were designed by William Kent.

Near to the main house is a fine medieval church, restored by William Butterfield, and a late 15th-century watermill, which forms a fine picture reflected in the water. The mill is set upon a small island by the side of the River Thames and it is possible to see it working and to purchase flour ground on-site. There is a tearoom in Mapledurham House if you wish for early refreshment.

When you have enjoyed all that is to be seen in the village, retrace your steps past **The White House**. In about ¼ mile, head left up the driveway towards **Bottom Farm**, passing the farm buildings and taking a footpath to the right of **Bottom Plantation** – look out for red kites circling overhead.

By the end of the 19th century, human persecution had driven red kites to extinction in England. In the early 1990s, a small stock of the birds was imported from Spain and released in the Chilterns by the RSPB and English Nature.

Continue on the footpath into **Long Ground Plantation** and go up the clear track through the trees. At the junction of paths, bear right up a delightful avenue of laurels to emerge on a good bridle-path – there is a superb black and white thatched cottage to your right called **Holly Copse Cottage**. Bear left and ascend past **Briar Cottage** and proceed up a tarmac driveway. The driveway becomes a lane and then a hedged footpath that leads past **Waterfield Nursery** to a lane

by an old post office. (2 miles)

⑤ Go left along the lane for 150 yards then turn right over a stile, following the waymarker direction and passing a large pool. Then continue by the side of the hedge to a further stile onto a lane. Head left along this lane past **Copyhold Farm** to reach the edge of **Hill Bottom** village. Bear right onto the top road to reach the **Sun Inn**. (1¼ miles)

⑥ From the inn, continue up the main street. Immediately after passing **Box Cottage**, turn right up **Cashes Lane** and ascend into the

woodland called **Great Oaks**. The footpath arcs left through the trees and, after about 250 yards, you reach a junction of paths. Bear left, exiting the trees onto a footpath that curves westwards, with the buildings of **Great Oaks School** over the hedge to your right. After walking through the field of wild flowers, you pass through woodland to reach the **B471** road. Cross over the road and continue along a lane, going in a westerly direction. The lane enters trees where bluebells add colour in the spring. At the track junction bear left. This track arcs to the right and joins a lane and heads towards **Stapnall's Farm**

THE SUN INN AT HILL BOTTOM

– the farm has been converted to stables. Just before reaching the driveway to **Chalkward Cottage**, go left through a white gate, cross over a field, and then go through a hand-gate in the far right-hand corner to stroll along a delightful footpath through the trees of **Great Chalk Wood** – lovely walking through bluebells and blackberry plants. Initially you pass through the middle of the woodland and then go along its left edge to arrive in the open. At the driveway to **Gatehampton Farm,** head left along a fenced track/tarmac lane that has a pleasing view to your right over the Thames and the railway. As the track reaches trees, it curves right and then, where it bends left, you go right, down the signed **Chiltern Way** path – a sort of hedged gully going generally west. In about ¹/₂ mile you reach a junction of paths and a track. Here you go left through a kissing gate into a nature reserve and ascend a hillock for a very fine view over the

River Thames and the surrounding countryside. As you descend the other side of the hillock, you go over a stile into the woodland of **Hadstock Nature Reserve**, then descend to the **Thames Path.** (2¹/₂ miles)

⑦ Here, turn left to join the National Trail. Walk this good footpath through the trees and you will be able to enjoy glimpses of the river to your right. After about ³/₄ mile the path arcs gently left away from the river and you will arrive in open countryside on a hedged footpath. This leads onto a farm track that has become a private lane and you follow this as it curves gently southwards past several farms and a stables. Eventually you will arrive at the **B471** road on the outskirts of **Whitchurch-on-Thames**. Cross over the **B471** and head to the left on the raised footpath. After 550 yards, cross over the road to the war memorial. (2 miles)

Date walk completed:

LOWER SHIPLAKE AND THE RIVER THAMES

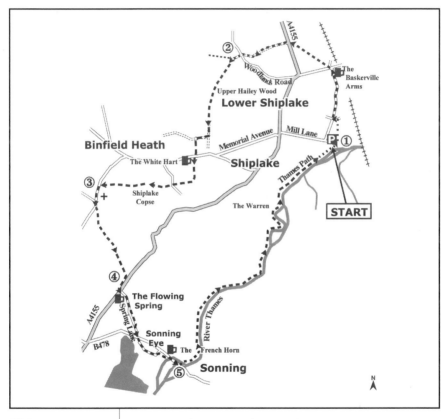

Distance:
8¹/₂ miles

Map: OS Explorer 171 – Chiltern Hills West

Starting point:
Mill Lane near to
Shiplake Lock.
GR 775788

How to get there: *Lower Shiplake is 2¹/₂ miles south of Henley-on-Thames. Take the A4155 road from Henley, passing to the west of Lower Shiplake. Go left into Mill Lane and you will find parking space towards the end of the road.*

*A*n interesting small town, lovely woodland, attractive villages, a fine pub, a beautiful bridge and the Thames Path are all encountered on this easy walk and, together, make for an adventurous day out. Early August is a particularly interesting time because that is when the annual Wargrave and Shiplake Regatta is held and you can enjoy the impressive sight of oarsmen battling on the famous river. The walk starts near Shiplake Lock, taking you into Lower Shiplake and wooded areas before descending to Binfield Heath village. Good tracks/footpaths lead to the Flowing Spring, where refreshments can be had. Quiet lanes and footpaths continue to Sonning Eye, where you will see a very fine old bridge and join the Thames Path. The walk is completed with a stroll along the towpath of a stretch of the meandering River Thames.

The Flowing Spring can hardly be bettered as a place to refresh the inner parts on a warm summer's day, as you sit on the upper balcony, which is dressed with beautiful hanging baskets, or in the large, well-kept gardens. A pint and a wholesome, home-cooked meal make this a piece of paradise. The landlord provides a warm welcome to walkers in this traditional country pub where there is plenty of room, with comfortable seating for diners and drinkers alike. Children are permitted inside and can also enjoy a small play area within the large garden.

Food and drinks *are available throughout opening hours. The pub is open at lunchtime on every day of the week from 12 noon until 2.30 pm and in the evening on Wednesday through to Saturday from 6.30 pm to 9 pm (no evening opening on Sunday, Monday or Tuesday).*
Telephone: 0118 969 3207; fax: 0118 969 6718.

 *The Walk*

① Walk to the end of **Mill Lane** to reach the **Thames Path**. Proceed ahead for about 10 yards then go left up a fenced footpath across open land. At the end of the field bear left and go over a stile, then bear left again onto a private road that leads to **Mill Road**. Here, turn right and head up the road into **Lower Shiplake**.

Shiplake and Wargrave are two

124

ALONG THE THAMES PATH

small villages set either side of the River Thames. The Wargrave and Shiplake Regatta is a special occasion, being attended by oarsmen from all over the world. It is one of the largest regattas on the Thames, with races for skiffs, punts and canoes attracting over 600 individual competitors to 350 races over two days. The boats are traditional in style and heavy, being similar to the craft used in Victorian times, but they remain superb racing machines. The skiffs are clinker built, double sculled, fixed pin and seat, and coxed.

They are sculled by combinations of first timers, local veteran gentlemen and Olympic and university oarsmen. There are events for all age groups.

Shiplake is associated with a number of famous people. Its church is where Alfred, Lord Tennyson (1809–1892) was married and Jerome K. Jerome mentions it in his book Three Men in a Boat. *George Orwell published his first work,* Awake Young Men of England, *while he was living in Shiplake. He also lived in Henley-on-Thames and went on to write* Animal Farm *and* Nineteen Eighty-Four.

At the main road junction (the **Baskerville Arms** is on the corner) proceed ahead, following the direction of a bridleway sign up **Northfield Avenue** – a no-through-road. This will lead you along a peaceful residential road and you will pass a number of attractive houses as you walk in a generally north-westerly direction. Soon you will be walking on a fenced footpath to reach the **A4155** road.

Cross over the **A4155**, with care, and continue up the bridleway opposite. This is a wide, tree-lined lane and after about 1/2 mile you

cross over **Woodlands Road** to follow the path signed 'Mays Green 1'. (1 3/4 miles)

② After some 100 yards the lane/track arcs right and here you go left along a clear footpath across a cultivated field into **Upper Hailey Wood**, which you enter over a stile. Proceed along the path through the trees. Initially the path hugs the right-hand edge of the woodland but then curves left into the trees. Exit the trees onto a hedged track and, after 200 yards, turn right along a track. In a further 160 yards head left through the hedge onto a waymarked footpath set to the left of the field hedge, until you reach a

SHIPLAKE LOCK

road with the **White Hart** pub to the right opposite. Cross over the road and continue along the footpath set to the left of the pub. This clear path commences in a southerly direction across a cultivated field, and then bears right, crossing over a minor road. As you progress along the path you will enter **Shiplake Copse** over a stile and walk through the superb bluebell woods.

These bluebell woods turn into golden beech woods in autumn, providing delightful country walking. Look out for deer, foxes and badgers, but do keep an eye on the sky too because red kites are regular visitors.

Exit the woodland via the stile and continue to the right of the field hedge over a couple of fields until you arrive at the road in **Binfield Heath**. (1³/₄ miles)

③ Go to the left along the side of the quiet road and after about 200 yards you will pass the Congregational church (founded in 1825). At the bend in the road, bear left onto a hedged track. Bear left again at the junction of tracks and then descend gently towards the **A4155** road. This track that you are on becomes a lovely hedged track with attractive wild flowers adding to the charm. (1 mile)

④ At the road, head to the right along the permissive path to the right of the road hedge and, after about 200 yards, go left down the timber steps onto the **A4155** road. Cross over the road to arrive at the **Flowing Spring**. From the inn, proceed down the lane to the left of the pub, taking care because this otherwise quiet lane appears to be used by motorists as a short-cut. After about 100 yards, bear left off the lane and continue along **Watto's Walk** – a footpath just to the left of the lane hedge. After ¹/₄ mile, the Walk brings you back onto the lane and soon you reach the **B478** road. Cross over the road with care, and proceed through the gateway opposite onto a dead-end minor road. Head left along the road until you reach a private house. Just after arcing left, go right (almost ahead) and you will soon be walking on a fenced footpath along the back of the houses. Eventually you will emerge by **Furleigh Cottage** near to the **French Horn** (a hotel/restaurant). Proceed up to the **B478** road and go along the road pavement over **Sonning Backwater Bridges** – an attractive stretch of walking, with a mill building set to your right. (1 mile)

Take your time to enjoy delightful Sonning, linked by the beautiful Sonning Bridge to Sonning Eye. In his Three Men in a Boat Jerome K. Jerome describes Sonning as 'the most fairy-like little nook on the whole river'. The Deanery in Sonning is one of the finest houses by the architect Sir Edwin Lutyens (1869-1944), who also designed Queen Mary's dolls' house at nearby Windsor Castle. The garden was laid out by his frequent collaborator Gertrude Jekyll. It was first owned by Edward Hudson, founder of Country Life magazine. The Mill at Sonning, an 18th-century flour mill, has been converted into a theatre.

⑤ Cross over the **B478** road just before the traffic lights and head left over the footbridge across the **River Thames** to arrive on the **Thames Path** on the west side of the river.

The Thames Path follows England's best known river for 184 miles as it meanders from its source in Gloucestershire through rural countryside into the bustling city of London. As you walk the Thames Path, you will pass peaceful water meadows rich in wildlife, historic towns and many lovely villages set in a landscape of gentle, wooded hills – there are many fine houses to admire. From the superb 18th century hump-backed bridge at Sonning,

the ever widening Thames continues on its way to London.

Proceed along the Thames Path for the next 2³/₄ miles. You will pass near to **Shiplake College** in **Shiplake** and will see its church up amongst the trees.

Shiplake College enjoys a unique riverside location and you may see some of the students working with their boats. The following quotation from R. C. Lehman in 1909 is of interest:
'In a college like Oxford or Cambridge, rowing does for those who practise it nearly everything that the rules of the authorities propose to do. It makes them lead a regular and simple life; it gets them out of bed early in the morning and sends them to bed again at ten at night; it disciplines them, it keeps them healthy, for it makes temperance necessary... If I could only add that it forces a man to his books and necessarily made him a brilliant subject for examiners, I should have compiled a fairly complete list of academic virtues.'

All too soon you will reach **Shiplake Lock**, where you bear left to return to **Mill Lane**. (3 miles)

Date walk completed: